How to Design a Program Evaluation

Carol Taylor Fitz-Gibbon
Lynn Lyons Morris

Center for the Study of Evaluation
University of California, Los Angeles

SAGE Publications
International Educational and Professional Publisher
Newbury Park   London   New Delhi

Copyright © 1987 by The Regents of the University of California

The second edition of the *Program Evaluation Kit* was developed at the Center for the Study of Evaluation, Graduate School of Education, University of California, Los Angeles.

The development of this second edition of the CSE *Program Evaluation Kit* was supported in part by a grant from the National Institute of Education, currently known as the Office of Educational Research and Improvement. However, the opinions expressed herein do not necessarily reflect the position or policy of that agency and no official endorsement should be inferred.

The second edition of the *Program Evaluation Kit* is published and distributed by Sage Publications, Inc., Newbury Park, California, under an exclusive agreement with The Regents of the University of California.

For information address:

SAGE Publications, Inc.
2455 Teller Road
Newbury Park, California 91320

SAGE Publications Ltd.
6 Bonhill Street
London EC2A 4PU
United Kingdom

SAGE Publications India Pvt. Ltd.
M-32 Market
Greater Kailash I
New Delhi 110 048 India

Printed in the United States of America

Library of Congress Cataloging-in-Publication Data

Fitz-Gibbon, Carol Taylor.
    How to design a program evaluation / Carol Taylor Fitz-Gibbon,
Lynn Lyons Morris.
        p. cm. —— (Program evaluation kit ; 3)
    Bibliography: p.
    Includes index.
    ISBN 0-8039-3128-X (pbk.)
    1. Educational evaluation—United States—Planning.
2. Educational surveys—United States—Planning. I. Morris, Lynn
Lyons. II. Title. III. Series: Program evaluation kit (2nd ed.) ;
3.
LB2822.75.F57 1987
379.1′54--dc19   87-16495   95 96 97 98 99 21 20 19 18 17 16
                     CIP

Contents

Acknowledgments 7

Chapter 1. An Introduction to Evaluation Design 9

Designs in Summative Evaluation 11

Designs in Formative Evaluation 14

Evaluation Where Design Presents Problems:
Programs Aimed at Special Populations 20

For Further Reading. 24

Chapter 2. The Elements of Design 25

Groups 25

The Times at Which Measurements Are Made 35

Selecting a Design 48

Chapter 3. Designs—An Overview 55

The Notation Used for Diagramming Each Design 55

Design 1: The True Control Group, Pretest-Posttest Design 56

Design 2: The True Control Group, Posttest Only Design 57

Design 3: The Non-Equivalent Control Group,
Pretest-Posttest Design 58

Design 4: The Single Group Time Series Design 58

Design 5: The Time Series with a Non-Equivalent
Control Group 61

Design 6: The Before-and-After Design 62

Major Threats to the Implementation of Designs 62

For Further Reading 64

Chapter 4. Designs 1, 2, and 3: The Control Group Designs 65

Design 1: The True Control Group, Pretest-Posttest Design 65

Design 2: The True Control Group, Posttest Only Design. 80

Design 3: The Non-Equivalent Control Group,
Pretest-Posttest Design 86

For Further Reading. 96

Chapter 5. Designs 4 and 5: The Time Series Designs 97

Design 4: The Single Group Time Series Design 97

Design 5: The Time Series with a Non-Equivalent
Control Group. 114

Chapter 6. Design 6: The Before-and-After Design 117

Design 6: The Before-and-After Design 117

**Chapter 7. A More Complex Design: Analysis of
Variance (ANOVA)** 128

Summary 137

For Further Reading 139

Chapter 8. How to Randomize 140

The Unit of Analysis Problem 140

Random Assignment of Students, Classrooms, or
Schools to Programs 144

Selecting a Random Sample 161

For Further Reading. 165

References 166

Index 167

Acknowledgments

The preparation of this second edition of the Center for the Study of Evaluation *Program Evaluation Kit* has been a challenging task, made possible only through the combined efforts of a number of individuals. First and foremost, Drs. Lynn Lyons Morris and Carol Taylor Fitz-Gibbon, the authors and editor of the original Kit. Together, they authored all eight of the original volumes, an enormous undertaking that required incredible knowledge, dedication, persistence, and painstaking effort. Lynn also worked relentlessly as editor of the entire set. Having struggled through only a revision, I stand in great awe of Lynn's and Carol's enormous accomplishment. This second edition retains much of their work and obviously would not have been possible without them.

Thanks also are due to Gene V Glass, Ernie House, Michael Q. Patton, Carol Weiss, and Robert Boruch, who reviewed our plans and offered specific assistance in targeting needed revisions. The work would not have proceeded without Marvin C. Alkin, who planted the seeds for the second edition and collaborated very closely during the initial planning phases.

I would like to acknowledge especially the contribution and help of Michael Q. Patton. True to form, Michael was an excellent, utilization-focused formative evaluator for the final draft manuscript, carefully responding to our work and offering innumerable specific suggestions for its improvement. We have incorporated into the *Handbook* his framework for differentiating among kinds of evaluation studies (formative, summative, implementation, outcomes).

Many staff members at the Center for the Study of Evaluation contributed to the production of the Kit. The entire effort was supervised by Aeri Lee, able office manager at the Center. Katherine Fry, word processing expert, was able to accomplish incredible graphic feats for the *Handbook* and tirelessly labored on manuscript production and data transfer. Ruth Paysen, who was a major contributor to the production of the original Kit, also was a painstaking and dedicated proofreader for the second edition. Margie Franco, Tori Gouveia, and Katherine Lu also participated in the production effort.

Marie Freeman and Pamela Aschbacher, also from the Center, contributed their ideas, editorial skills, and endless examples. Carli

Rogers, of UCLA Contracts and Grants, was both caring and careful in her negotiations for us.

At Sage Publications, thanks to Sara McCune for her encouragement and to Mitch Allen for his nudging and patience.

And at the Center for the Study of Evaluation, the project surely would not have been possible without Eva L. Baker, Director. Eva is a continuing source of encouragement, ideas, support, fun, and friendship.

—Joan L. Herman
Center for the Study of Evaluation
University of California, Los Angeles

Chapter 1

An Introduction to Evaluation Design

A *design*[1] is a *plan* which dictates *when* and *from whom* measurements will be gathered during the course of an evaluation. The first and obvious reason for using a design is to ensure a well organized evaluation study: all the right people will take part in the evaluation at the right times. A design, however, accomplishes for the evaluator something more useful than just keeping data collection on schedule. A design is most basically a way of gathering *comparative information* so that results from the program being evaluated can be placed within a context for judgment of their size and worth. Designs reinforce conclusions the evaluator can draw about the impact of a program by helping the evaluator to predict *how things might have been had the program not occurred* or if some other program had occurred instead. The comparative data collected could include how the school environment might have looked, how people might have felt, and how participants might have performed had they not encountered the particular program under scrutiny. Usually a design accomplishes this by prescribing that measurement instruments—tests, questionnaires, observations—be administered to comparison groups *not receiving the program*. These results are then *compared* with those produced by program participants. At other times, predictions about what would have happened in the program's absence can be produced without a comparison group through application of statistical techniques.

The objective of this book is to acquaint you with the ways in which evaluation results can be made more credible through careful choice of a design prescribing when and from whom you will gather data. The book helps you choose a design, put it into operation, and analyze and report the data you have gathered. The book's intended message is that attention to design is important.

Even if choice or practicality dictate that you ignore the issue of design, it is important that you understand the data interpretation options which you have chosen to pass by. In the majority of evaluation situations, *some* comparative information is better than none. Your choice of a design will perhaps determine whether the information you produce is believed and used by your evaluation audience or shrugged off because its many alternative interpretations render it unworthy of serious attention.

The book's contents are based on the experience of evaluators at the Center for the Study of Evaluation, University of California, Los Angeles, on advice from experts in the field of educational research, and on the comments of people in school settings who used a field test edition. The book focuses on those evaluation designs which seem most practical for use in program evaluation. Please be aware that these are *not the only* designs available for adoption as bases for useful research. They do seem to be, however, the most straightforward and intuitively understandable. This makes them likely to be accepted by the lay audiences who will receive and must interpret your evaluation findings. Please bear in mind, in addition, that many of the recommended procedures in this book prescribe the design of a program evaluation *under the most advantageous circumstances.* Few evaluation situations exactly match those envisioned here or described in the book's myriad examples. Therefore, *you should not expect to duplicate exactly suggestions in the book.* Evaluation is a relatively new field, and correct procedures, even where choice of a design is concerned, are not firmly established. In fact, while considerable attention has been given to the quality of measurement instruments for assessing cognitive and affective effects of programs, relatively little attention has been paid to the provision of useful designs. Your task as an evaluator is to find the design that provides the most credible information in the situation you have at hand and then to try to follow directions as faithfully as possible for its implementation. If you feel you'll have to deviate from the procedures outlined here, then do. If you think the deviation will affect interpretation of your results, then include the appropriate qualifications in your report.

If political pressures or the heat of controversy make it important that you produce credible information about program effects, few things will support you better than a well chosen evaluation design. Often evaluators discouraged by political or practical constraints have chosen to ignore design, perhaps cynically deciding that a good design represents information overkill in a situation where little attention will be paid to the data anyway. The experience of evaluators who have chosen to use good design has been to the contrary. The quality of information provided through use of design has often *forced* attention to program results. Without design, the information you present will in most cases be haunted by the possi-

bility of reinterpretation. *Information from a well designed study is hard
to refute*; and in situations where they might have been ignored or
shrugged off because of many or ambiguous interpretations, conclusions
from a good design cannot be easily ignored.

The *Program Evaluation Kit,* of which this book is one component,
is intended for use primarily by people who have been assigned the role of
program evaluator. The job of program evaluator takes on one of two
characters, and at times both, depending upon the tasks that have been
assigned:

1. You may have responsibility for producing a *summary statement* about
   the effectiveness of the program. In this case, you probably will report
   to a funding agency, governmental office, or some other representative
   of the program's constituency. You may be expected to describe the
   program, to produce a statement concerning the program's achievement
   of announced goals, to note any unanticipated outcomes, and possibly
   to make comparisons with alternative programs. If these are the features of your job, you are a *summative evaluator.*

2. Your evaluation task may characterize you as a helper and advisor to
   the program planners and developers or even as a planner yourself. You
   may then be called on to look out for potential problems, identify areas
   where the program needs improvement, describe and monitor program
   activities, and periodically test for progress in achievement or attitude
   change. In this situation, you are a "jack of all trades," a person whose
   overall task is not well defined. You may or may not be required to
   produce a report at the end of your activities. If this more loosely
   defined job role seems closer to yours, then you are a *formative
   evaluator.*

The information about design contained in this book will be useful for
both the formative and summative evaluator, although the perspective of
each will vary.

Designs in Summative Evaluation

Typically, design has been associated with summative evaluation. After all,
the summative evaluator is supposed to produce a public statement sum-
marizing the program's accomplishments. Since this report could affect
important decisions about the program's future, the summative evaluator
needs to be able to back up his findings. He therefore has to anticipate the
arguments of skeptics or even the outright attacks of opponents to the
conclusions he presents. While good design won't immunize him against
attack, it will strengthen his defense. Historically, designs were developed
as methods for conducting scientific experiments, methods through which
one can logically rule out the effect on outcomes of anything other than

the *treatment* provided. In the case of educational evaluation, this treatment is an educational program. Since designs serve the interest of producing defensible results, and since such production is primarily the interest of the summative evaluator, you will find throughout the book a strong summative flavor in both the procedures outlined and the examples described.

To readers who are working right now as evaluators, the suggestion that *design* is of critical importance for summative evaluation may seem a little off-base. "No one uses experimental designs," you might say. "No one uses control groups." And you would be nearly correct, unfortunately—at least with regard to large Federal and State funded programs. Not long ago a study of a nationwide sample of ESEA Title VII (Bilingual Education) evaluations revealed that *no one* attempted to use a *true,* randomized control group, and only 36% tried to locate a non-randomized control group for comparison with any aspect of the programs evaluated (Alkin, Kosecoff, Fitz-Gibbon, & Seligman, 1974). In another study, a search of 2,000 projects that had received recognition as successful located not one with an evaluation that provided acceptable evidence regarding project success or failure (Foat, 1974).

The reasons for this state of affairs are no doubt legion, but four come up frequently:

1. *Funders seem to view programs as one-shot enterprises.* Once a program has been implemented and has run its course, it becomes a *fait accompli.* It's over. Summative reports, then, describe something that has already happened. They are seldom seen as a chance to describe programs and their effects in the interest of future planning. In order to testify that a program took place *at all,* a summative report need not use a design. Designs become valuable only when someone hopes to use information about program processes and effects as a basis for future decisions such as whether to pay for similar programs or to expand the current one. Designs are *essential* when someone has in mind the development of theories about what instructional, management, or administrative strategies work best.

2. *Evaluators are called in too late.* This problem is actually a common symptom of the first. Evaluation often occurs as an afterthought. Lack of careful planning in the establishment of the program removes the possibility of a carefully planned evaluation. The evaluator finds that he has no control over the assignment of students or the sites chosen for implementation of the program. The evaluator has to "evaluate" an already on-going program. While this situation does not eliminate the possibility of obtaining good comparative information, it usually makes use of the best designs impossible.

3. *Because of ethical and/or political concerns, it is often difficult to accomplish the most rigorous designs.* Social programs often are aimed

at individuals or groups in great need, and withholding potential program benefits from some for the sake of a comparative research design can be hard to justify. In addition, it is frequently the case that politics rather than social science methodology determines where or for whom special programs will be implemented, precluding opportunities for randomized designs.

4. *Social science research in general is still in its youth.* Lack of research design in evaluation stems partly from its relative novelty as a method for gathering social science information at all. Sir Ronald Fisher's work in statistics and design, an essential methodological step forward for the social sciences, was completed in the 1930s! Not very long ago.

5. *Educational researchers and evaluators themselves cannot agree about the appropriateness of research designs for evaluation.* While most writers in the field of evaluation concur that at least a part of the evaluator's role is to collect information about a program, the nature of the rules governing data collection are still debated. Opponents of the use of design usually list as major drawbacks the political and practical constraints discussed here already, and the technical difficulties involved with using the findings from one multifaceted program to predict the outcomes of others.

Defenders of design, the authors of this book among them, acknowledge these problems. They continue to urge the use of design in field settings because designs yield the comparative information necessary for establishing a perspective from which to judge program accomplishments. In fields of endeavor such as education, where clear absolute standards of performance have not been set, comparison is a way to subject programs to scrutiny in order eventually to determine their value. Nonetheless, some of these impediments to good design are more intractable than others. Suggestions are offered at the end of this chapter for optimizing those situations where there are significant intractable constraints.

Summative Evaluation and Educational Research

Summative evaluations should whenever possible employ experimental designs when examining programs that are to be judged by their results. The very best summative evaluation has all the characteristics of the best research study. It uses highly valid and reliable instruments, and it faithfully applies a powerful evaluation design. Evaluations of this caliber could be published and disseminated to both the lay and research community. Few evaluations of course will live up to such rigid standards or need to. *The critical characteristic of any one evaluation study is that it provide the best possible information that could have been collected under the circumstances, and that this information meet the credibility requirements of its evaluation audience.* The best interpretation of your task as summative evaluator is that you must collect the most believable information you can, anticipating at all times how a skeptic would view your report. Keeping this skeptic in mind, set about designing the evaluation which has potential for answering the largest number of criticisms.

The aim of the *researcher* is to provide findings about a program which can be generalized to other contexts beyond it. Criteria for what constitutes *generalizable* information have been agreed upon by the social science community; they are the topic of educational research texts. Though it is important as a service to education that the *evaluator* provide such information if the situation allows good design and high quality instrumentation, the evaluator can usually limit his projection of the quality of data he must collect to what he perceives will be acceptable to his unique audience. It is not beyond the scope of the evaluator's job, however, to *educate his audience* about what constitutes good and poor evidence of program success and to *admonish them* about the foolishness of basing important decisions on a single study—or even a few. It is equally within the summative evaluator's task to *advocate,* based on his information, *changes* in a program or in funding policy or to *express opinions* about the program's quality. The evaluator who takes a stand, however, must realize that he will need to defend his conclusions, and this again means good data and a well designed study.

Designs in Formative Evaluation

All this discussion about design in summative evaluation should not persuade the evaluator that design is irrelevant in the formative case. The use of design during a program's formative period gives the evaluator, and through her the program staff, a chance to take a good hard look at the effectiveness of the program or of selected subcomponents. This enables the formative evaluator to fulfill one of her major functions—to persuade the staff to constantly scrutinize and rethink assumptions and activities that underly the program. Careful attention to design can also help the formative evaluator to conduct small-scale pilot studies and experiments with newly developed program components. These will inform decisions among alternative courses of action and settle controversies about more or less effective ways to install the program.

The message to the formative evaluator is this: Including a source of comparative information—a control group or·data from time series measures—in any information-gathering effort makes that information more interpretable. Too often formative measurement happens in a vacuum; no one can judge whether students are making fast enough progress, for instance, because no one can answer the question "Compared to what?"

Example 1. Franklin Elementary School has designed a pull-out program in reading for slow readers and wishes to assess the quality of the progress of the students during the program's first year of operation. The hope is that students in the pull-out program will make faster progress because of increased attention. The problem is knowing what pace to expect from slow students. The vice-principal, serving as program evaluator, has located a school in the same district which uses the same programmed readers which form the backbone of the pull-out program—the O'Leary Series. The evaluator has persuaded the principal of the other school to allow her periodically to test their slow readers for comparison with Franklin's. The evaluator has constructed a test using sample sentences from the O'Leary series which will be administered for oral reading by both the pull-out program students and the students in the other school. Since it is the first year of the pull-out program, information gained from comparing the two schools will be used formatively. If Franklin's readers are not progressing faster than the controls, then this might signal a need for modification in the pull-out program. The design here is Design 5, the Time Series with Non-Equivalent Control Group, described in Chapter 5.

Example 2. Osirus High School designed a six-week career awareness module for the tenth grade based on field trips in which all students spend one afternoon a week at the work places of professionals pursuing careers in which the students are interested. The students conduct interviews and write short biographies describing each professional's route to success. Due partly to the extreme cost of such a large-scale field program, the school's director of vocational education decided to do some formative evaluation, assigning students randomly to the first six-week program tryout. This provided a Design 2 evaluation (Chapter 4) since no pretest was given. At the end of the six-week module, an achievement test revealed that students had acquired large amounts of information about the careers of their choice, and were able to write essays which the career education staff judged to be realistic appraisals of the economic and social accompaniments to these careers. Students also seemed to have acquired a good sense of the steps necessary to attain an education toward the career of interest. A look at the control group, however, showed that students who had *not* taken part in the career education program had acquired the same information and the same set of realistic expectations simply through talking to students who were taking part in the field test. It seemed that it might not be necessary for every student to go into the field every week—at least this didn't seem critical for making cognitive gains.

For formative evaluation, it is a good idea at the outset to locate or assemble a control group, as described in Designs 1, 2, and 3, or to collect time series measures before the program begins (Designs 4 and 5). Laying down even the rudiments of design will give you a chance to make comparisons in order to interpret your findings or to justify your formative recommendations if you should need to.

Because of the nature of your job, you can try using designs for formative evaluation in several ways, according to your own discretion:

1. *You might set up as "controls" various alternative versions of the program you are helping to form.* You may be able to identify alternative versions that the program can take, possibly one or more less costly or time-consuming than the others. You could set up two or more versions in different schools or classrooms, some receiving the more expensive or more lengthy alternative. These alternatives could vary in the amount they differ from the basic program, as well as in their duration. They could last a short time, say, until someone has determined their relative quality; or they could span the duration of the whole program, providing you at the end with an assessment of their— and its—overall effectiveness. If whole schools or classrooms received the alternative version, your evaluation would comprise a Design 3 study (Chapter 4), an evaluation with a non-equivalent control group. If you have programs going on in several different classrooms to which you can randomly assign students, you can implement a true control group design. Often the "control group" tends to be thought of as a set of losers, people who unluckily miss out on all the good benefits of the program. In a design which sets two competing versions of the program operating at the same time and where each of them is equally viable and potentially effective, exactly which group is the experimental group and which the control is really not worth considering.

***

Example 1. A junior high school language arts teacher is in the process of designing a writing curriculum for seventh and eighth grades. Realizing that motivation is a strong determiner of junior high performance in any topic, the teacher has come up with four ways to motivate students to write; but of course he doesn't know which will work best, or if some will work better with some students than others. To give him this needed information for future planning, he has decided to perform a formative evaluation using one of the different strategies in each of his four roughly comparable, heterogeneously grouped classes: one group will edit its own magazine; another will write articles to be submitted to popular national magazines; a third group will write letters to the editor of the local newspaper; and a fourth group will write a play about the problems of adolescence. The teacher hopes to take further advantage of this instance of Design 3, the Non-Equivalent Control Group Design (Chapter 4), by analyzing results on periodic writing exams separately for students whom he assessed to be good or poor writers in the first place.

Example 2. A soap manufacturer wants to market a new stain remover for delicate fabrics. The marketing division has several ideas for how to promote the new product: coupons for a reduction in the price of the product, small free samples mailed to consumers' homes, and medium-sized samples to be sold at a reduced price through grocery stores. Past experience with such promotions is insufficient to determine which strategy would work best with this particular product. In order to decide which promotion idea is best, the marketing division selects three small equivalent test markets comprising similar consumers and then implements each of the promotion ideas with a different test market. The results of this initial promotion together with cost data will help the company decide which promotion works best and should be used in the nationwide marketing campaign.

Example 3. A district-wide Early Childhood Education program has decided to incorporate a psychomotor development component that will require installation of large playground equipment. In order to answer many questions about the best way to integrate the program into the overall early childhood curriculum, the district's Assistant Superintendent for Early Childhood Programming has decided to install the equipment in two-week phases to groups of randomly chosen schools. The entire pool of the district's elementary schools will be divided randomly into eight groups. The groups will receive the equipment and begin the program at two-week intervals. Having eight groups begin using the materials in this stepwise fashion will give the staff a chance to do formative evaluation. After administering a pretest, they will work with Group 1 for two weeks and then administer a psychomotor unit test. They will make necessary program modifications, then initiate the program with Group 2. Group 2's pretest results, because of randomization, should match Group 1's. Results of the unit test with Group 2, however, can be *compared* with results from Group 1 to determine if program modifications have had an effect on student development. This revision/program installation/test cycle can repeat as many as six more times, or until the program seems to be yielding maximal gains. This useful formative design is actually a version of Design 1, the True Control Group Pretest-Posttest, detailed in Chapter 4.

Tempered by proper caution about the danger of basing extremely important decisions on studies with small numbers, "formative planned variations" allow you to rest program planning on more than hunches.

2. *You might relax some of the more stringent requirements for implementing a design.* Since formative evaluation often collects information for the sole use of program staff, the formative evaluator can, where necessary, relax some of the requirements for setting up a design. This means that, when necessary, you can use assignment of students that is slightly less than random, or choose a non-randomized control group from students of a somewhat different socioeconomic group, *as long as interpretation of results is accompanied by appropriate caution.* The formative evaluator can at times relax design constraints because the formative evaluator's constituency is the program staff. They will

use the data he gathers to make program change decisions. They will, in addition, serve not only as judges of what constitutes credible information but they will, through constant contact with the program, gather much of their own data—at least that concerned with attitudes and impressions. In situations when the formative evaluator has been able to set up comparison trials of various program versions, staff members inevitably gather firsthand experiences to use as a basis for making program revisions.

Regarding design, the job of the formative evaluator seems to be to provide many opportunities for comparison, using as good a design as possible. The details of the implementation of any one design are not critical.

Example 1. Jackson Elementary School, in the heart of a large urban area, received Federal funds to design a compensatory education program for the middle grades, with a particular focus on basic skills. The school identified the students eligible for the program according to the state's requirements for receiving the funds. By and large, these students were chronically low achievers. A young and devoted school staff had ideas about how best to use the money: they installed an Enrichment Center based on open school guidelines, and used much of the money to hire classroom aides. They were interested in keeping close watch on the quality of achievement that their first year of program operation produced, but they could not locate a control group. Someone suggested that the students in the school who traditionally performed slightly below average but not as poorly as the target students might form a rough control group for the study. Subsequently the decision was made that these students would be tested for progress in reading, math, and writing at the same times and using the same pre and post measures as the program students. This is a modification of Design 3, the Non-Equivalent Control Group Design (Chapter 4), with a special awareness that the control group is indeed non-equivalent. The control group, for one thing, did score just significantly higher than the program students on a standardized pretest. A careful watch over the course of the school year, however, showed that program students received extensively more attention in basic skills areas and at the end of the year were achieving about the *same* as the control group. Such a design helped the staff conclude that the new program indeed did benefit the target students: they were now achieving as well as students who had scored better than them in the past.

Example 2. A toy manufacturer planned to start a daycare center for its employees' children and wanted to monitor the program's effect on employee absenteeism. Since the company could not randomly assign employees to use the daycare center, it had to use a non-equivalent control group. In this case, the company focused its evaluation on the employees in one particular department. Prior to the opening of the daycare center the evaluator collected baseline data on absenteeism for all parent-employees in the selected department who were potential users of the center. Data was collected again after nine months of program operation from two groups of employees: (1) the parents in the selected division who were using the daycare program and (2) the remaining parents in the selected division (with similar jobs and similar numbers and ages of children) who were not using the center (either because they preferred alternate care arrangements or were on the new center's waiting list). In this way the company was able to determine that the new daycare program did in fact cut down on the absenteeism of employees who used the program while the absenteeism of the other, similar employees was not significantly reduced.

An exception to this pronouncement about formative evaluation and more relaxed designs occurs in the case of controversies within the staff over different versions of program implementation. One of the jobs of the formative evaluator is to collect information relevant to differences of opinion about how the program should be designed or implemented. In this case, as with summative evaluation, challenges to the conclusiveness of results can occur, and credibility will become again important. Disagreements among planners can be translated into alternative treatments to form bases for small experiments designed according to the guidelines in this book.

3. *You might want to perform short experiments or pilot tests.* You will find that program planners must constantly make decisions about how a program will look. Most of these decisions must be made in the absence of knowledge about what works best. *Should all math instruction take place in one session, or should there be two during the day? How much discussion in the vocational education course should precede field trips? How much should follow? Will reading practice on the Readalot machine produce results as good as when children tutor one another? How much worksheet work can be included in the French course without damaging students' chances of attaining high conversational fluency?* You can settle these questions by believing whoever offers the most convincing opinion, or you can subject them to a test. Using one of the evaluation designs described in this book, particularly Designs 1, 2, or 3, you can conduct a short study to resolve the issue. Read Chapters 2 and 3. Then choose treatments to be given to students (or whomever) that represent the decision alternatives in question. The duration of the short study should last as long as you feel will realistically allow the alternatives to show effects. If you will be reading this book for the purpose of designing short experiments, please substitute the word *treatment* for *program* as you read the text. The designs described in the book, and the procedures outlined for accomplishing them are, of course, equally appropriate.

Example 1. A group of third grade teachers attending a convention heard about a mathematics game which they thought would teach multiplication tables painlessly if played every Friday morning. Interested in saving their students the agony of drill, the teachers urged their principal to purchase the game. The principal, a former math teacher, was skeptical of the value of what she called "playing bingo." She refused. The teachers, however, persuaded the principal to agree to a test: they would randomly distribute students among their four classrooms every Friday morning for four weeks, carefully controlling the number of high and low math ability students distributed to each classroom. Two of the teachers would play the math game; the other two would drill their students in the same multiplication tables, and give prizes for knowing tables exactly like those to be won playing the game. At the end of the month, the data would be allowed to speak for themselves. This highly credible Design 1 study would uncover differences between drill and the program if any were to be attained.

Example 2. A survey research organization has a contract to collect nationwide data on school staffing for the U.S. Department of Education. The data will be collected via written surveys of principals and teachers at thousands of schools. In order to manage such a large data collection effort and ensure the integrity of the sample via a very large return rate, the research organization is considering using a school employee at each site as a survey coordinator. Agency staff disagree on the feasibility of this plan and on whether or not it is necessary to pay the survey coordinator in order to achieve a high response rate. With so much at stake, the research agency has decided to field test the entire procedure as well as the instruments. In the field test it will randomly assign its sample of schools among the three proposed methods of managing the data collection task: no on-site survey coordinator, a volunteer coordinator, and a paid coordinator. In this way the research organization can compare rates of return and difficulty of securing responses so as to select the best way to do the eventual nationwide study.

Use of design requires planning in advance, if only to locate a group that is willing to serve as the comparison. Even if you have no intention of collecting comparative data at the outset, it might be a good idea to locate a handy group from whom you will be able to pull students in order to try out new lessons or plans or to do short experiments. Often you will find a teacher who is not taking part in the program who will be glad to provide you with a little time to give supplementary instruction, a short quiz, or a questionnaire to his class.

Evaluation Where Design Presents Problems: Programs Aimed at Special Populations

Many evaluators find themselves in the position of collecting information about the quality of funded programs aimed at helping students, clients, or others who are extremely rich or poor in a certain disposition, ability, or attitude. In a school setting, for example, these special categories of children might score, for instance, in the top 2% on an IQ test and be labeled gifted, or below 75 IQ and be classified as retarded. The students may be handicapped or emotionally disturbed. Programs aimed at these students present unique design problems because laws requiring that all such children be educated rule out evaluation designs where the control group receives *no* special program. A comparison group can therefore only be formed if the school has *two* special programs available for special students.

> **Example.** A school tried two different kinds of programs for its gifted students. Gifted students were randomly assigned to one or another program for a 10-week trial period, at the end of which benefits from both programs were assessed by the principal. Reactions of students and parents were positive for both programs, but one program involving field trips raised considerable resentment from students not in the program. Since they were unable to justify the field trips as necessary, the principal and staff chose to continue with the other program.

The following paragraphs suggest other possible approaches to evaluation of special education programs. The reader is also referred to *How to Use Qualitative Methods* (Volume 9, *Program Evaluation Kit*) for a discussion of alternative approaches.

1. *Use the Non-Equivalent Control Group Design* (Design 3, Chapter 4). Such a comparison could be made if another district or school with no special programs, or programs appreciably different from yours, agreed to give the same tests as yours and to share results.

> **Example.** Teachers of educable mentally retarded students planned a reading skills program which they hoped would significantly improve the reading of their EMR students. They asked a nearby elementary school to share with them results of a reading test given by the district in May each year and to permit a criterion-referenced test to be given to the EMR students at the beginning and end of the school year. Progress of the two groups in reading could be compared.

2. *Adopt a formative approach and evaluate program components.* Comparative studies of the effects of whole programs are not always the best service you can provide to the program staff or even the funding agency. Rather, more useful information can be gained by evaluating *components* of a special education program with a view to recommending changes that might be needed in these. In some cases, for example, alternative materials might be available for teaching the same objectives. Small-scale experiments could be set up in several schools, using a Pretest-Posttest True Control Group Design (Design 1, Chapter

4) in each classroom to obtain objective data on the effectiveness of the various alternatives.
3. *Compare diverse programs in terms of some common indicator,* such as satisfaction with program outcomes using Design 3. Sometimes an evaluator is asked to evaluate a number of special programs which individual schools or projects have produced and which all have different goals and objectives. For example, perhaps at one school the gifted program concentrates on acceleration in math, at another on breadth of exposure in science, at another on creative writing, and at a fourth on all these things at once. You could measure at all schools student and parent *satisfaction* with the instruction provided in individual subjects (math, science, writing skills). Perhaps you would find results like this:

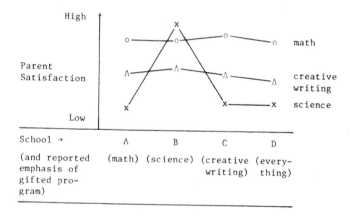

In general, parents seem equally satisfied with both math and creative writing, no matter what the emphasis reported by the school. Satisfaction with science, however, seems very sensitive to whether or not science is emphasized by the gifted program. When it is, there is high satisfaction. The evaluator might note that in the absence of special effort, science might *not* be well taught to gifted students, at least if parent satisfaction is a valid indicator.

The point of this example is that diverse programs can be assessed if you can find a single dimension on which to compare them. Opinions and attitudes often provide this common ground. This kind of investigation at least tells you what kind of programs seem to make a difference on the dimension you have chosen.

4. *Compare program outcomes to pre-established criteria* and use Design 6 (Before-and-After Design, Chapter 6). Frequently special programs are required to state measurable goals, and the evaluator's job is to measure

goal achievement. This often turns into a game of who can set goals which are lofty enough to be acceptable but simple enough to be reached, especially when goals are set in terms of standardized test gains. Sometimes, however, when the goals are derived from criteria which have intrinsic, recognizable value, reasonable goal setting is an excellent approach. For example, specification of some basic survival skills, such as reading road signs correctly and making change, for retarded students, could provide mastery goals for an EMR program. In a company wanting to improve the overall health of its workers, reasonable goals could be such basic measures of good health as blood pressure and weight within certain ranges. A fairly good assessment of program effectiveness can be made even in the absence of a good design, if program results can be compared to reasonable goals.

5. *Make the evaluation theory-based.* A good approach to assessing the results of special education programs is to do a *theory-based evaluation.* This is an evaluation that focuses on program *implementation,* holding the staff accountable for operating the program they have promised. The theory-based evaluation first asks, *On what theory of instruction, theory of learning, psychological theory, or philosophical point-of-view is the program based?* In other words, what activities does the staff view as critical to obtaining good results toward which the program aims? Detailed questioning of the staff makes explicit the model, theory, or philosophy that the staff is trying to implement. Once you know the staff's intention, your job will be to ascertain if activities that are specified by the theory are being effectively operationalized and implemented. Of course if you decide to do a theory-based evaluation, the existence of planned activities must be documented through objectively collected evidence, not just through testimonials. If you can show in your evaluation that the elements which the theory specifies as necessary for goal attainment are present, then you have shown that the program has taken an effective step toward goal achievement. If the theory is correct, goals should be reached eventually. For example, in the company's employee fitness program mentioned above, "health" is to be improved through a theory-based regimen of diet and exercise. Hence, the evaluator will focus on whether employees are actually being helped to implement certain prescribed dieting behaviors and allowed time at work to exercise three times a week.

NOTE

1. Some writers have used the word *model* instead of design, probably because the choice of such a measurement plan usually affects the evaluator's whole point of view about the seriousness of the enterprise and about how information will be gathered, analyzed, and presented. This book prefers *design,* the less ponderous term, and it will be used throughout.

For Further Reading

Anderson, S. B. (Ed.). (1978). *New directions in program evaluation.* San Francisco: Jossey-Bass.

House, E. R. (Ed.). (1973). *School evaluation: The politics and process.* Berkeley: McCutchan.

Morris, L. L., & Fitz-Gibbon, C. T. (1978). *Evaluator's handbook.* Newbury Park, CA: Sage.

Popham, W. J. (1975). *Educational evaluation.* Englewood Cliffs, NJ: Prentice-Hall.

Struening, E. L., & Guttentag, M. (1975). *Handbook of evaluation research* (Vol. 1). Newbury Park, CA: Sage.

Worthen, B. R., & Sanders, J. R. (1973). *Educational evaluation: Theory and practice.* Worthington, OH: Charles A. Jones.

Chapter 2

The Elements of Design

As was discussed in Chapter 1, a design for an evaluation is essentially a plan stating who will be measured (observed, or tested) and when; that is, which groups and at what times. This chapter describes these two elements of design, groups and times, and discusses some of the important considerations relevant to each. Table 1 on page 47 shows how several possible combinations of these elements fit together to make the six designs which will be presented in this book.

Groups

It should be noted right away that in talking about which groups are measured in evaluation designs, the word *group* is used in a special way, as an abbreviation for *treatment group*. A group of students, employees, or others means those who all get the same program or treatment. The experimental group consists of people who receive the experimental program. Occasionally, confusion arises about the meaning of group because of the word's other uses. For example, a person might say, "Two groups received the program; a group of boys and a group of girls." In terms of design, it would be better to say that the experimental group—those students who received the program—were classified as boys and girls. Sex was a classification factor. The word *group* is reserved for a collection of people *defined by the treatment or program they receive*. At times, group might refer to a group of classrooms or schools that have been selected for a program rather than to a group of individual students. In planning an evaluation, you will always plan to measure the *experimental group,* that is, the group (e.g., of students, classrooms, schools, employees, divisions) who receive the program which is to be evaluated. This book will frequently abbreviate experimental group as *E-group.*

Please be advised that in evaluations where *only* the experimental group is measured, interpretation of the results is difficult and often unconvincing. Without any *comparison* group, it is hard to know how good the results are, whether the results would have been as good with some other program, and even whether the program had any effect on the results at all. Consequently, it is strongly recommended that you use a comparison, or control, group.

The Control Group

A control group is a group consisting of persons who are as similar as possible to those in the E-group, and who are measured at the same times as the E-group, but who do not get the experimental program. This book will frequently abbreviate control group as *C-group*. The fact that the control group does not get the experimental program does not mean that the group gets *no* program. The question of exactly what kind of program the control group gets is considered in a section starting on page 29.

Control groups come in many varieties. Depending on the circumstances, a control group in educational evaluation might consist of, for instance, six individual students, or three different classrooms, or the school down the road, or the handicapped children in a neighboring school district. In a business setting, a control group might be several individual employees, half of all the clerk typists, or an entire division at a separate site.

The ideal situation is for the control group and the experimental group to be as similar as it is possible for two groups of people to be—identical in every way. In actuality, of course, control groups will be different from the experimental group to various degrees—some very different, some pretty similar. Trying to find out exactly *how* similar two groups are would be an interminable task. You could see if they were similar with regard to age, sex, verbal IQ, nonverbal aptitude, background, knowledge of basic skills, perseverance, attitude toward their job or school, cooperativeness, and so on. Many such characteristics *could* affect a person's reaction to a program.

Consequently, while the similarity between two groups might lie on continuum from very similar to very different, we do not attempt to assess this continuum. We simply divide control groups into two kinds: those made *equivalent* by random assignment which generally assures a non-biased distribution of the various characteristics, and those that do not employ random assignment and must therefore be considered *non-equivalent*.

The equivalent, or "true," control group

A *true* control group is one formed by random assignment. *Randomization is the way to make an equivalent, or true, control group.* The best evaluation design that you can implement—whether you are conducting a short experiment or an entire summative evaluation—is one employing a true control group. This is so because, in general, results that are gained from such a design are not likely to have been caused by anything other than the *difference in treatment* given to the experimental and control groups. Suppose, for example, that an evaluation has shown that Program X students (the Experimental group) on average had higher posttest scores than Program C students (Program C students form a control group). The results might be attacked as entirely unconvincing by such comments as:

"Well, the kids in Program X were smarter."

"That course did better because the parents of many children in that particular class are professionals."

"The control group started out lower than the group getting Program X so naturally they finished up lower."

Random assignment of people to programs is the most effective way of eliminating such explanations. Randomization avoids alternative explanations by making it likely, when two or more programs are to be compared, that factors which influence outcomes—smartness, home background, pretest level of achievement—will be evenly distributed to each program from the beginning. Random assignment of people to two programs, for example, will make the two groups roughly equally smart and of equal home background.

Randomization will also wash out all sorts of other factors you might never have considered, but which might influence results. For example, random assignment of people will evenly distribute those who live in the same neighborhood. This may turn out to be a neighborhood where, unknown to you in September, there will be a flu epidemic the following January, causing many lengthy absences. All those absences from *one* program might be devastating to its effects. If the flu affects *both* programs, then your evaluation is still in business since roughly the same number of people will be absent from both. You can still make the comparison at year's end. Neither program might accomplish all that it could have, but your ability to compare them will not be seriously impaired. And this comparison is the essence of your evaluation.

If it has occurred to you that randomization might be effective in equalizing groups when the numbers of people or teams involved are large, but is less likely to be effective as the numbers get smaller, you are correct. For very small groups (fewer than about 15 people or teams in *each* when you are making separate groups), special considerations for random assignment must be made. These considerations are discussed in Chapter 8, which describes procedures for the random assignment of people to groups.

In addition to the effect random assignment has on making groups equivalent, it is desirable for another, equally important reason: statistical tests of the results require that there be random assignment for their proper application and accurate interpretation.

Ways to achieve true control groups

Because randomization is the best way to eliminate alternative explanations for results you wish to attribute to a program, random selection or assignment of people or teams to programs is the most desirable way to design an evaluation. Designs using randomization are the best choice whether you are conducting a summative evaluation, a formative one that uses a comparison group, or a small experiment. Randomization ensures high credibility for whatever you report.

Although randomization is important to strong evaluation results, you might encounter resistance trying to use it in practical situations. People might object to random "chancy" assignment to programs which last a long time and are likely to greatly influence their lives. The following paragraphs suggest some strategies for overcoming common objections.

The two new programs strategy. Because new programs arouse interest and enthusiasm even though they may eventually turn out poorly, you may find it better to use a *second new program* as the control for Program X: randomly assign people to one new program or the other. This other "new" program could easily be a version of the first which subtracts or augments one of its more costly features. It could also be a true and altogether different competitor to the first. As was mentioned in Chapter 1, trying several competing programs yields valuable formative information, if you should need it. The evaluation will show which of the new programs was most effective, or if the feature you have removed or changed made much difference. Whether your evaluation is formative or summative, the strategy will, in addition, alleviate the political difficulties accompanying a no-program control group.

The borderline control group strategy. This strategy is appropriate when the people most in need *must* be given Program X, such as when Program X is a remedial program or a special program for a group with a special need. The measure of who is most needy is never perfectly accurate. There is almost always a large *borderline* group of people among whom it is difficult to decide which are the most needy. If scores on a particular test are being used to decide about who gets the program, the borderline people will be those whose scores fall within a few points of the cut-off score. In such a case, the non-borderline, most needy people must be assigned to Program X, but the borderline group can be randomly assigned to Program X or the control group. This allows for a thorough evaluation of the value of the program for borderline people—information that is especially pertinent to whether or not to expand the program. Procedures for forming a borderline control group appear on pages 156 to 157.

The taking turns strategy. Sometimes first one group and then another group can be given Program X. For example, an expensive new copy machine might be made available to a random selection of these departments for the first half of the year and then to those in the remaining three departments for the second half of the year. Because departments can be randomly assigned to their "turn," a true control group is achieved.

The delayed program strategy. Even though all people will eventually be given Program X, a strong evaluation of at least part of it can be obtained if the entry of a randomly selected group of people can be delayed. Starting out on a small scale is frequently justifiable and wise in implementing a new program anyway.

The delayed evaluation strategy. If Program X is already in operation so that it is too late to form an equivalent control group, use a less credible design this time and lay the groundwork for a good design the next time the program is tried.

The non-equivalent (non-randomized) control group

This is a group *selected* because it is similar to the experimental group. It is not formed by random assignment. Sometimes a non-equivalent control group is called a "comparison" group to distinguish it from a true control group. If random assignment is impossible, then you should try to find a group which is as similar as possible to the experimental group and use that group for comparison. Here are some examples of non-equivalent control groups.

Example 1. A junior high school started an accelerated mathematics program for a group of its twenty most able students. Anxious to control for regression effects (discussed on page 37 of this book) and to answer such questions as, "Did the students make better than usual progress?" the chairman of the math department asked a neighboring school to cooperate by allowing a few measurements to be made. Granted permission, he tested students at the neighboring school and selected their top twenty *by the same procedure he had used in his own school.* This group then became the non-equivalent control group. This group might well have differed in several ways, coming from a slightly different residential area and having attended a different school. However, a check of scores on a math pretest showed no significant difference between the groups on that measure, making the group quite desirable as a control. The similar math scores did not, of course, mean the groups were similar on all measures. Moreover, there were also many differences between what happened to the groups besides their different mathematics programs; that is, *confounding* was a problem. Nevertheless, such a non-equivalent control group proved useful.

Results of pre- and posttests on both groups showed that both groups gained well over a year on a standardized math test and there was no significant difference between mean scores. However, the experimental group was also able to write quite complicated computer programs. They had "kept up" with their peers and profitted from the enrichment provided by the special program. If the evaluation had shown only that the accelerated students had learned some computer programming, the charge could have been leveled that the learning had been at the expense of more routine mathematics achievement. The comparison with the control group dispelled this challenge. *The non-equivalent control was well worth using!*

Example 2. The Rockport School District implemented a policy of returning educationally handicapped (EH) children to regular, hetero-geneously grouped classrooms in the elementary schools. A goal of this program was increased positive attitudes toward school on the part of the EH students. The district administrators were anxious to find what effect this policy change in fact had on these attitudes and requested a formal summative evaluation. The evaluator considered the surrounding school districts and asked two of them to cooperate in exchanging data on EH students. One district was adjacent, but of slightly higher SES. The other district was selected because, although farther away, the income levels and assessed valuation of property were very close to Rockport's. Toward the end of the year, a random sample of EH students from each district was interviewed by a psychologist who was not informed of the purpose of the study nor of the difference in programs. She rated students on their attitude to school, self-concept, and so on. Her results showed that only 40% of those interviewed from Rockport showed a strongly positive attitude toward school. This result might have seemed discouraging, but results from the other two dis-tricts (the non-equivalent control groups) showed that only 15% and 20% had positive attitudes toward school. The use of non-equivalent control groups was again worthwhile: *they showed what the results might have been without the program.*

Example 3. A fastfood restaurant in a shopping mall revised its menu and began selling salads and other alternatives to hamburgers. A goal of the revised menu was to capture a larger share of the mall business. In order to determine whether increases in business volume actually reflected a larger share of the market or simply a temporary or seasonal increase in mall customers overall, the restaurant owner tried unsuc-cessfully to convince another similar restaurant to share data. Eventu-ally, the restaurant owner was able to persuade an ice cream store to share information on changes in its number of customers during the time period in question. The restaurant owner realized that the volume of ice cream sales in the mall might be affected by some variables dif-ferent from those affecting his own business such as weather and changes in the competing dessert stores, so he collected some informa-tion about these variables to help explain the results. This comparison of the changes in his business volume with those of the ice cream shop provided a better estimate of whether his revised menu was actually having the intended effect.

As you can see from these examples, the collection of data from a non-equivalent control group can be helpful in assessing the effect of a program and therefore worth attempting in situations in which a true control group cannot be formed. While valuable for summative evaluation, a non-equivalent control group from another school, district, or other organization can provide an easily obtainable basis of comparison for formative evaluation as well. It allows you to avoid the problem of randomly depriving local employees or customers of the program, while still providing a means to judge the quality of program progress with respect to others.

Remember these three points about non-equivalent control groups:

1. If the experimental group is selected by means of a particular procedure (e.g., a math pretest in the first example and EH placement in the second example), then the control group should be selected by a procedure which is as nearly the same as possible.

2. The non-equivalent control group should be given all the major tests that the experimental group is given. In this way, they too become accustomed to the style and content of the tests. The testing can itself make a difference to achievement; *so unless curriculum-embedded unit tests are an integral part of one of the programs,* the experimental and control groups should both get the same tests throughout the program. This will be important if there are frequent tests to be given during the program in addition to the usual pretest at the beginning and posttest at the end.

How can testing affect achievement? Tests do the following:

- Focus the students' attention on important parts of the curriculum
- Give the students practice on the kinds of items that will likely constitute the final test
- Affect motivation by providing students with knowledge of how well they are doing, if results are made available
- Point out to the teacher areas of weakness in the instruction so they can be corrected

Having the same testing program for both groups is, of course, equally important when there is a *true* control group. When the control group is at another school, as is frequently the case with non-equivalent control groups, however, this rule about equal testing is often violated.

3. Be prepared to document similarities and differences between the control and the experimental groups. The credibility of your findings will depend on your ability to demonstrate that the experimental and control groups have been *as alike as possible except for the difference in the programs they received.* Think of all the ways a skeptic could cast doubts on the appropriateness of the non-equivalent group. For example, she might say, "Class sizes were different," "The hours spent on the subject were different," "The nursery school those kids attended

taught phonics," or "The E-group was of higher SES." Check out any serious problems by collecting relevant information and examining it.

What program should the control group get?

Something will obviously happen to the control group (the C-group) each day during the time when the E-group participates in Program X. Presuming that you will have some say about what happens to the control group, what should that something be? This section lists the possibilities, considering the best solution first and working down to the weakest, though even the weakest solution, be assured, is much much better than no control group at all. The discussion which follows applies to both true and non-equivalent control groups and to all three information-gathering situations in which you might employ designs—summative and formative evaluation and the conducting of short experiments.

The best solution. Remembering that evaluations are conducted to provide information for decisions, it is clear that the best solution is one which provides the most useful information for whatever decisions have to be made. Though this is seldom explicitly stated, if you think about it, the evaluation of a program is conducted in order to *choose between Program X and some other course of action*—having no program at all, or implementing a program other than Program X as it currently looks. Ideally it is a representative of this other action, either no program or Program X's *closest competitor*, which the control group should receive.

Example. A district committee examined sex education materials with a view toward adopting a set of materials for use in a new sex education program. They narrowed their selection down to two possible sets of materials. Some members of the committee felt one set of materials, while good, was too explicit and would evoke negative reactions from parents. Other members of the committee felt that the explicit materials were the best, that there would not be objections to them, and that the alternative materials were too evasive. It was decided both sets of materials should be tried out and student and parent reactions assessed. Fifth and sixth grade classrooms at several schools were randomly assigned to use either the explicit or the evasive materials. At the end of the tryout, questionnaires were sent to parents and given to students. From these data, the impact of each program was assessed and an informed choice could then be made.

It is important to note that the closest competitor might not be *another* program, but a cheaper or less time-consuming version of the program being evaluated.

The next best solution. If you cannot implement what you consider to be a truly competing program for the control group, then at least it would be good if the control group were to get a program which had aims and objectives similar to those of Program X. This control program might be the old program even though you don't expect that you will continue the old program. Perhaps, for example, you plan to just keep looking for a better program. It still pays to keep the old program running a year or two while you try out new ones. How else will you know whether or not the old program was in fact *better* than any of the new ones you try? It is possible, after all, that in spite of innovations, the old program still produces the best results.

In other situations the control program might be a program you have never tried and do not intend to.

Example. A large corporation wanted to improve the results achieved by its employee alcohol abuse program and planned to implement some revisions. The old program consisted merely of a counselor who referred employees to various outside treatment programs. In the new program the counselor would be extended to full-time so that he could also work out leaves or reduce work loads to facilitate the employees' maintaining their positions while receiving treatment for their alcoholism. The new plan would also add weekly on-site group support meetings during paid work hours. Even though the company did not plan to continue the original program, it decided to keep it in one site for a year while the new one was being implemented in a second site. To determine whether the new program was a significant improvement over the existing one, the two company sites were compared. The sites were selcted on the basis of roughly comparable rates of employee alcohol problems and several work-force characteristics such as number of employees, age range, and ethnic composition.

A weak solution. Sometimes you might only be able to compare the experimental group, which uses a special program, Program X, with a control group which gets *no program at all.* This arrangement might be the only one possible even though "no program" is *not* a course of action being considered. "Is a comparison between Program X and no program worth making?" you might ask. The answer is certainly *yes.* It does permit a test of the program, even though a weak one, one where the program is not too likely to fail. It enables you to decide whether the program is better than no program at all. And, in cases where the possibility may arise, it allows you to detect whether or not Program X has done any harm.

Example. In the elementary school of a partially bilingual community, a random selection of sixth grade students (the E-group) was provided with programmed Spanish language materials to work on during study periods. Periodically throughout the school year, these students were tested on their knowledge of the basic Spanish in the programmed texts. Along with them, an equal number of other students (the C-group) was also tested. As expected, the control group students scored poorly compared to the E-group since they had no special program. However, their scores provided a *baseline* from which to judge the scores of the E-group. They showed how well the E-group performed compared to people who had picked up some Spanish informally. What is more, both E- and C-groups were tested in math, the subject most often worked on during study periods. No difference was found between the groups, so the conclusion could be made that devoting some study time to Spanish caused the E-group students no damage.

The example above illustrates how the no-program group yields a baseline from which to judge the results of the program. Provision of the baseline is another important reason why even a no-program comparison is worth making. The comparison "controls for" the effects of *maturation*. That is to say, it takes into account the fact that students get older and pick up information simply with the passage of time. At the end of many programs, particularly year-long programs, you do not know whether students are scoring higher than they did at the beginning because of the program or because they are "older and wiser."

The rapid intellectual growth during the early elementary years makes this problem particularly serious when evaluating elementary school programs. *The skeptic could argue that program children are doing better simply because they would have matured and learned anyway.* They would be just as far along without the program. By measuring another group which did not get the program, you get an idea of how much of the increase in scores is attributable to the students' growing up. A good program should produce more maturation.

An important point must be made about the interpretation of comparisons made between E-group results and C-group results. If both groups get programs which have *exactly the same* goals and objectives, then each program is subjected to a stringent test: Can it compare favorably against a true competitor? If, however, the C-group gets a program which has a somewhat *different* emphasis from the program the E-group gets (for example, math Program C might not spend as much time on basic computational skills as Program X, preferring to introduce more abstract concepts), then interpretation of different results is more difficult. If Program X cannot produce higher scores on content which represents *its own* greatest emphasis, then Program X does not seem to be doing too well—it cannot win on its own ground, so to speak. It is a good idea to make this comparison; the other program's performance provides a kind of lower limit of acceptable results.

This focus on Program X's results is sufficient if you are evaluating Program X only; but if you want to discuss the value of *both* programs, more effort will be required. You can simultaneously evaluate both Program X and C in two possible ways:

1. Report *three* sets of results, one set for each program's major distinct goals and one set for goals held in common by the two programs. Or,

2. Ask an independent expert to select the most important objectives or test items and use this selection as the basis for designing or choosing an outcome measure for both programs.

The discussion about what should happen to the control group boils down to one basic idea: Program X can be subjected to a strong or weak test depending upon the kind of control program to which it is compared. The closer the control program is to the alternative(s) being considered, the more useful the evaluation for future decisions. These ideas are summarized in Figure 1.

The Experimental Group: A Few Words About the Program It Should Get

Though the experimental group should, of course, receive the experimental program, it is important that you remain vigilant to the *quality of its implementation.* An evaluation or even a short experiment, after all, is a *test* of the effectiveness of an educational treatment. Everyone, therefore, should be concerned that the program be implemented at its best and strongest. If the wrong materials are used, or if instruction is halfhearted or cut short, then lack of significantly stronger impact over the control group will be hard to interpret. It is often difficult for educational interventions to show strong results in any case. To maximize the likelihood of the program's making an impact, you should urge the program staff to keep its best foot forward throughout the evaluation.

At the beginning of this chapter it was stated that a design is a plan stating *who* is measured, and *when.* So far, this discussion has focused on who is measured: groups.

The Times at Which Measurements Are Made

Tests given before a program or an experiment starts are called *pretests,* short for pre-program tests. Similarly, tests given at the end are called *posttests.* Tests might also be given several times before, during, or after a program. These various possibilities will be discussed.

Posttests

Posttests are measurements made most usually at the end of a program or an experiment. It is in the posttest scores that the results should show. The posttest is the *dependent variable*; the posttest results *depend,* partly at least, upon what happened in the program.

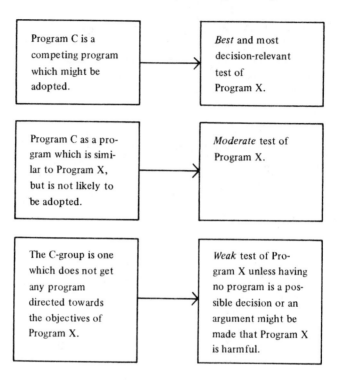

Figure 1. Summary of possible comparison groups for evaluating an experimental program

Because posttests measure the results of a program, designs never omit the posttest altogether, although occasionally only part of a group takes the posttest. There are often practical questions, however, which determine exactly *when* a posttest occurs. Sometimes, for instance, the date of a posttest is dictated by when a report on the program is due. In this case, set the posttest date so that you leave yourself twice as much time as you figure you will need for the preparation of the report! However, if the report is not due until well after the program ends, you can be more flexible in choosing when to give the posttest.

In a program that spans a school year, you will want to give the program time enough to produce maximum results, but you should also recognize the restlessness which begins to set in before summer vacation. This June restlessness might mean that you will get a better measure of the program in May than if you wait until the very end of the school year. Measurements in other types of organizations or businesses may be subject to perturbations at particular times of the year depending on the nature of the business, its work force, and customers, such as deadlines at the end of a fiscal year or tax year or seasonal changes in consumer spending. Your judgment and that of your staff will be your best guides about exactly when to give the posttest.

A further consideration in scheduling is the need for *make-ups*. Students or employees absent on the test day should take the make-up test immediately upon their return to school unless you and the staff feel that by then the content of the test would have become general knowledge, unfairly affecting results. In such a case, students not taking a particular test should simply not be counted in the data analysis. These omissions would be reported as test "mortality." If make-ups are to be given, the test must be scheduled early enough to allow subsequent time for make-ups.

Pretests: When to Use Them

Any test score or measurement which is collected *before the participants receive the program or began the experiment* can be called a pretest. You might want to use some kind of pretest in order to:

- Select people
- Check assumptions which have been made in planning a program
- Check on or ensure the comparability of groups
- Provide a basis for checking the gains made during a program
- Get a more sensitive test of a program's effects

Pretests to select people for the program

Sometimes people are selected for a program, or are eligible for a program, on the basis of the scores they have obtained on a test.

> **Example 2.** Secretaries were selected for a special computer training program if they could type more than 70 words per minute and scored above 90% correct on a math computation test.

In the second example, the typing and math tests were the *selection measures*. Having a score above particular levels was the *criterion* for selection. It is tempting to use the selection test as a pretest in subsequent analysis of program results. But beware: If a group of participants was selected because of extreme scores (high scores or low scores) on a test, the scores of that group will *regress toward the mean* on a subsequent test. In other words, the scores of a group of participants who were selected because they were very high will be lower on a retest, even with no teaching or learning intervening! The scores will change in this deceptive way because some participants, especially those near the cut-off point for the selection, produced an extreme score because of luck. On a retest, these participants will probably not have luck quite so with them again. Some of their scores will go down; some scores may even jump up considerably. All in all, the mean of the group may well fall. When you select the top of a group, they sometimes have nowhere to go but down. Statisticians call this move in extreme scores upon retesting *regression or regression toward the mean.*

In the case of participants selected on the basis of low scores, if they were given the test again, their mean score would most likely be higher. Again, there is regression toward the mean. In this case the participants selected for low scores included some who produced them because of careless errors or bad luck, such as guesses which came out wrong. With a few lucky guesses on a retest, their scores will improve.

It is clear that regression effects can affect the evaluation of a program. Remedial programs can falsely appear to be successful and gifted or accelerated programs can falsely appear to be unsuccessful, simply because of regression effects. For this reason alone, *it is very important to have a control group of some kind when evaluating remedial or accelerated programs* or any program for which participants were selected because of extreme scores. What is more, if this control group will be a non-equivalent one, it is important that group members come from a school or work and home background similar to program members. This is because extremely low scoring participants from generally high achieving groups can be expected to actually regress *more* toward the mean upon retesting than those from disadvantaged backgrounds. A case can be made that the low scorers from the advantaged environs were probably more unlucky when taking the selection test. The same reasoning applies to high scorers from disadvantaged backgrounds on tests for giftedness. They will be expected to regress more on retesting compared to a more advantaged control group with the same initial selection scores.

Recommendation: When a test is used to select students for a program on the basis of either high or low scores, it is best to give a *second test* as a pretest. The second test will not be subject to the same regression effects, and the scores on it are more likely to be normally distributed so that statistical tests will be appropriate.

Pretests to check assumptions which have been made in planning a program

A pretest is sometimes desirable as a check on the proper implementation of a program. Regarding almost any program, the question can be asked, "Are the actual participants those specified by the program plan? Is the program going to the people for whom it was intended?" A pretest can be used to check such things as the pre-program achievement or attitudes of the students and staff to be involved.

Example 1. A bilingual program was planned based on the assumption that most Spanish-surnamed students spoke Spanish at home. A pretest indicated that this was not so. This necessitated some modifications in the program.

Example 2. An elementary school math program was planned assuming that children who knew multiplication tables could also add numbers fluently. But a pretest based on the program's elementary math objectives showed that some children who did well on items relating to multiplication were nevertheless still very poor at addition. The hierarchical order of instruction which had been planned had to be modified. Some children apparently do not learn things in the expected sequence!

Pretests used to check on or to ensure the comparability of groups

If the *posttest* scores of two groups are to be compared, the first question that must be cleared away is whether the groups were similar to *begin with*—before one group got Program X and another got Program C, or before the experiment began. If you are using a true control group, that is, if the two groups were formed by random assignment, there might be no need for such a check as long as the number of people involved is fairly large.[1] Randomization should have worked to make the groups reasonably equivalent. However, if the numbers to be assigned were small, then randomization might be less successful in equalizing the groups. In this case, you should use a pretest to see if randomization has produced groups showing no appreciable difference.

Better still, however, is the practice of *using a pretest to assist the randomization*. Using this method, a pretest is given to all. Blocks of high scoring, medium scoring, and low scoring people are formed, and members of each block are then randomly assigned to the experimental or control program. These procedures are described more fully in the section on "Blocking" in Chapter 8.

If you are using a non-equivalent (non-randomized) control group, a pretest is *essential* to check whether the control group and the experimental group are initially comparable.

Recommendation: In the case of a true control group, random assignment reduces the need for a pretest, but use one to ensure equivalent groups if the numbers involved are small (less than about 15 per group) or if the variability is very large (e.g., I.Q.'s range from 70 to 120). Always use a pretest if the control group is non-equivalent (non-randomized). The pretest should be an equivalent form of the posttest, or if this is not possible, should measure a skill known to be related to the posttest measure.

Pretests used to check the gains made during a program

You do not know how far you have come if you do not know where you were to begin with. Similarly, without a measure of how things were before a program started, you will not be able, when the program finishes, to point to gains which have been made. If evidence is required of precisely what has been learned or gained in a program, then this is a good reason for using a pretest. Such evidence is obtainable and interpretable, however, *only when criterion-referenced tests*[2] *are used.* When actual test content is *not* going to be a consideration, as, for example, when a standardized test will comprise the posttest, a pretest is not essential and *the use of gain scores should be avoided.* The unfortunately common practice of basing evaluations on computation of standardized test gain scores—posttest score minus pretest—communicates very little about what students learned.

Example. A writing skills program was instituted for eighth graders. Basic writing skills were identified and grouped as objectives. At the beginning of the year, every student was tested on 20 objectives. Instruction proceeded in small groups composed of students who had not yet mastered subsets of the objectives. At the end of the year, all students were retested on the 20 objectives. Gains made by each student in terms of which objectives were mastered were reported to parents who had indicated that they wanted such information.

In cases where you are using a *true* control group, initial skills of both groups can usually be *assumed to have been equivalent* due to randomization. The comparison which must be made is between *the posttest scores from the E-group and C-group.* In such a case, only posttest scores are needed to answer the question: Did one program result in greater gains than another? Unless you are concerned that small numbers or high variability of scores might render even randomly composed groups non-equivalent, you need not pretest!

If you are using a non-equivalent control group, a pretest will be necessary. And in the case of formative or summative evaluations where there is *no control group,* a criterion-referenced pretest based on program objectives is essential so that gains can be documented.

The employees in a small business all attended a series of workshops on office communications. During the week prior to the program they each kept a diary of the number and contents of memos they wrote and received as well as the frequency, length, and topics of staff meetings they attended. In addition, they filled out a short questionnaire on their opinions about communication in their office. The same types of measures were taken again at the end of the program. Progress was thus measured not against a control group but rather against the treatment group's own baseline data.

Pretests to increase the sensitivity of your test of a program

In some cases you might have reason to suspect that the program you are evaluating or the short experiment you are conducting might not make a very dramatic difference in outcomes. If you want to be sure to detect whatever small difference is produced, then what you need is a "powerful" design. Having a pretest which is very closely related to the posttest will add to the power of your design.

Power as used here is a technical term. Statisticians probably selected the word with the analogy of a magnifying glass in mind. The more powerful a magnifying glass, the smaller the things you can see with it. Similarly with designs: the more powerful a design, the smaller the differences you can detect between two sets of results. With a powerful magnifying glass you can detect a difference between two ants which you could not have noticed with a less powerful glass. With a powerful design, you can detect a difference between two programs that, with a less powerful design, might have appeared to be insignificant.

A design has power to detect subtle differences when it enables the evaluator to explain the causes of variations in results—how much was contributed by individual differences, how much by errors, and so on. The way to increase the power of a design is to be able to explain more of the variation in results by measuring accurately at the outset the things that are likely to influence the results.

Example. Forty children who regularly attended an after-school play group applied to a camp for which there were only 20 places. The camp director randomly selected 20 students to go to the camp for two weeks. At the end of two weeks, he thought the camp children appeared to have lost weight. He weighed both the campers and the non-campers when they were all back in the after-school program. There was almost no difference between the mean weights of the children, but he thought this was due to the fact that some quite heavy children had gone to camp. He thought, "If I'd had an accurate measure of each child's weight before camp, I could see whether or not camp had made a difference, even a small difference, in children's weights." He asked children how much they had weighed before camp, but could not rely on the results of memory and of bathroom scales of dubious accuracy, and anyway, many children had no idea.

The camp director was quite right. He could have had a more powerful test of his hypothesis if he could have known more, explained away more of the variation in final weights as being due to *initial* differences in weight. Then he could have seen if camp children had indeed lost some weight. He was also correct in seeing that a measure with a lot of errors in it—like the results of asking children what they thought they weighed before camp—would not increase his power much.

As far as pretests are concerned, the greatest power can be obtained by having a pretest as similar as possible to the posttest. This is because a major contribution to how the person will score on the posttest is what she knows about the subject matter now. The best predictor of a person's future behavior of any kind is his present behavior in similar circumstances. Applying this very sensible principle to testing, the *best predictor* of what a child will be able to do in the future on a certain kind of test is the score he receives on that test now. The more accurately you can predict posttest scores from pretest scores, the better you will be able to detect deviations from the predicted scores, deviations possibly due to the effects of the program being evaluated. Thus, *using a pretest which is very much like the posttest* (both tests measure the same arithmetic skills, for example, or both tests measure spelling words of equal frequency or difficulty) *gives the most precise information about the effectiveness of one program compared with another.* Using maximally similar pre- and posttests increases the power of the evaluation design. It can render indisputable a true control group design in which such a pretest is used for blocking, and it can increase the credibility of even a design that includes no control at all.

Pretests: When Not to Use Them

The previous section discussed five reasons why you might wish to use a pretest. As you will have noticed, use of a pretest may be unnecessary when a true control group is part of the design. Below are some reasons why you might not want to use a pretest.

Don't use a pretest if taking a pretest would be likely to alter the students in some unmeasurable way. This might be the case if the posttest is to be a measure of attitudes. There is evidence that the act of stating one's attitudes, as one is sometimes forced to do, for example, when answering a questionnaire, can itself affect those attitudes. It can set them or make the student more vigilant about them, unpredictably affecting subsequent changes. Furthermore, the pretest of attitudes might alert students to the aims of a program or experiment and produce bias in their responses to it.

In spite of these reasons for *not* measuring attitudes prior to a program or an experiment, one would always like to know what the attitudes were, and there is a neat solution available if you have large enough numbers of respondents. If there are at least 30 respondents in each group, you can measure the pre-program attitudes of a *random half* of students who get the program. The post-program attitudes of the half who were not pretested will not have been influenced by any pretest-induced bias. Here is an example of this procedure.

> **Example.** Math teachers hoped that a new math program being implemented in an entire high school would improve students' liking for math as well as improve their skills. Before the program began, they prepared two kinds of questionnaires. One asked about mathematics (How much do you like it? Is it fun?), and the other asked about reading. The questionnaires were evenly mixed up in a pile and then randomly passed out to students so that about half the students answered a math questionnaire and the other half answered a reading questionnaire. Toward the end of the program the same questionnaires were readied for use again. The names of those who had answered the *reading* questionnaires were entered on blank *math* questionnaires. The other names were put on the reading questionnaire. In this way, when the named questionnaires were passed out, students who had previously been asked about math were now asked about reading and vice versa. This procedure provided a pretest measure and posttest measure for both math and reading. The math results were analyzed to check the impact of the new math program. The reading results incidentally provided a measure of a general attitude trend in another subject area, information which might assist in the interpretation of math results.

Don't pretest when using one would be meaningless. For example, if you were about to put in a new program involving the teaching of French, there would be no point in giving a pretest in French to an English-speaking group of children. Their scores would presumably be simply due to guessing; the pretest would not provide meaningful information. Alternatively, a language aptitude test, or some other test expected to correlate with the outcome measures, could be used as a pretest.

You may not wish to use a pretest because the program is already in progress and no pretest was given. You can't turn back the clock to interject the appropriate pretest for a program that is already underway. Do not, however, think that because no pretest was given you have lost access to information useful for interpreting results. Since *ability* measures are not supposed to be affected much by instructional programs, you could give an ability or aptitude measure as a *retrospective pretest.* Even though this measure is administered to the E-group and the C-group in the middle of the program, you should be able to assume that its scores represent the relative standing of the two groups before the program started. This assumption is more likely to be valid if the ability measure is a so-called culture-fair or non-verbal ability test rather than a conventional ability test containing considerable amounts of reading and arithmetic, skills the program might have influenced.

Finally, you may not wish to use a pretest because of the cost in time or money.

Pretests: Summary of Remarks

The following section summarizes the major principles you should remember regarding pretests. You will have noticed the following possible uses for pretests:

* A pretest may be an attitude test
* A pretest may be an achievement test
* A pretest may be an ability test

A pretest which is an attitude test. This occurs most often when the program or experiment aims at attitude changes. Because of the possibility that the pretest may itself influence attitudes or affect the way in which people respond to the program and/or to the later posttest, it is sometimes recommended that, within each group, only a random half be given the attitude test.

A pretest which is an achievement test. If the posttest is to be an achievement test, then the use of a pretest which is the same as or similar to the posttest gives valuable current status information, lending increased power to a design. Furthermore, the achievement pretest is a relevant measure on which to base a judgment about whether or not two groups are equivalent. A check on the equivalence of groups will be especially important if one of the following situations exists:

* There is a non-equivalent control group—always have a pretest if the control group was not formed by random assignment
* Small numbers, say less than 15 per group
* Large variability in the population being sampled—for example, if the groups selected contain a large ability range

A pretest which is an ability test. When the posttest is to be a measure of *achievement,* a measure of *ability* is often used as a pretest. This allows you to relate posttest scores to student ability levels. Such a comparison is often an excellent way to obtain a judgment of the *educational* significance of differences in posttest scores. The effect of the program can be compared with the effects of different levels of ability.

Example. At the end of an experiment to evaluate the effectiveness of parent tutoring in multiplication tables, it was found that the experimental group scored 10 points higher, on the average, than the control group. No one was quite sure how good a result this was until a teacher pointed out that, in the control group, the difference in scores between students of below average ability (90 IQ average) and students with above average ability (110 IQ) was about 10 points. This gave added information to help interpret the effects of the program: Students of below average ability who had received the program were performing like students of above average ability who had not received the program.

Using an ability measure as a pretest will not give as much power as that given by a pretest that is equivalent to the posttest. This is because an ability test will not usually be as closely related to the posttest results. For example, you would be able to make a better prediction of a student's arithmetic percentile at the end of a year if you knew his arithmetic percentile at the beginning of the year than if you only knew his IQ. An ability measure as a pretest will prove useful in several situations:

- When knowledge of the effect that ability level has on posttest scores will help you to interpret the size of the difference that the program has made, as depicted in the example above
- When a subject matter pretest is not possible due to the fact that the subject matter will be totally new to most students; this might occur, for example, with a beginning foreign language course or a training course in the use of a new machine
- When the posttest will be an attitude measure and you think attitudes might differ among ability levels as they usually do
- When the program has already started and no pretest has been given to either the program or control group; an ability measure can be used as a retrospective pretest

Tests Other than Pretests and Posttests

Mid-tests

You might wish to make some measurements during the time the program is running. These mid-program tests or mid-tests can indicate, for example, the impact of the program across time, as shown in the following examples.

Example 1. Management training scores of E-group and C-group from October to May

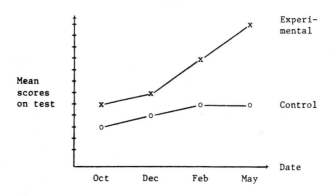

Interpretation: Off to a slow start, the experimental program produced better and better test scores as the program went on.

Example 2. Reading test scores of high and low ability students receiving Program X (no control group available)

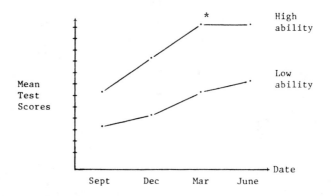

*This score indicates that high ability students had received maximum benefit from the program by March and could probably have undertaken other studies. Low ability students continued to make progress to the end of the year.

Mid-tests may be particularly helpful in both formative and summative evaluation when your evaluation design has no control group. In such a situation, you have to concentrate on examining the progress of the program being evaluated. Looking closely at its impact on different subgroups such as the high and low ability students in Example 2 is one way to accomplish this.

Retention tests

"They forget everything over the summer vacation" is not an unfamiliar comment, and it raises the whole problem of *retention*. A program which appears to teach students a great deal very quickly might look good next to a slower moving program on an end-of-the-school-year test. By the end of summer vacation, however, students from the two different programs might be indistinguishable in terms of what they can recall. What is more, one group might make more rapid progress once they got back down to work.

Recommendation: If Program X looks better (in terms of significantly higher scores of students) than Program C at the end of the school year, check the scores again in September by readministering the posttest after the long vacation. If it still looks better, you have a really good program! If the significant difference between the scores no longer appears, then withhold judgment and test again later.

"Time series" tests

When you begin to think about the extra information that retention tests give you beyond simply one immediate posttest, you note that single tests are not entirely satisfactory. A *series* of tests after a program finishes could check on long-term effects and detect whether benefits from the program are lasting or only transitory. A series of tests, usually given at equal intervals before and after the program, is called a *time series.*

A series of tests administered systematically before a program starts can actually eliminate the need for a control group. One problem with a before-and-after design, a design which has no control group, is that it is impossible to know what results might have occurred without the program. *A series of measures* made before the program starts can be used to project the results which would be expected if things had continued undisturbed. For example, given the results shown on the graph below for times 1, 2, 3, and 4, one could "predict" the result at time 6 using the extrapolation of the solid trend line indicated by the dotted line. Note that *at least three* measures are desirable in order to draw in the trend line. These three measures must be on the same instrument—for example, the same test or questionnaire or checklist.

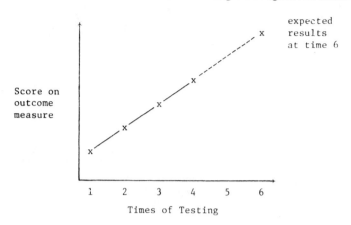

If, in addition, several measures can be collected after a program, then these measures will be of considerable assistance in determining whether its effects are stable.

Selecting a Design

This chapter has considered the two main elements of design—who gets measured and when. The designs in the following chapters represent in greater detail the various combinations of possible choices of the groups (who gets measured) and the timing of measurement (when). Table 1 shows how these elements can be combined to form the six designs discussed in Chapters 3 through 6 of this book. Each design presents three choices of groups to be measured:

- Experimental group only
- Experimental group and a true (randomly assigned) control group
- Experimental group and a non-equivalent (not randomly assigned) control group

And there are three choices for the timing of measures:

- Pretest and posttest
- Posttest only
- Time series—a series of, ideally, three measures before the program or experiment is implemented and three after it is finished

A thoughtful examination of Table 1 should help you tentatively select a design or designs for your summative or formative evaluation or for conducting a short pilot test. *Note that you may select more than one design for the same evaluation or experiment!* Each *instrument* could have a design of its own. For example, you may wish to do a posttest-only design for a measure of attitudes, a pretest-posttest design for a standardized measure of achievement, and a time-series design for a criterion-referenced achievement measure. Similarly, you might be able to locate easily an appropriate comparison group for part of the results of your program (for instance, regular training sessions for new employees in a company's own text processing system), but another part of your program (a one-time workshop for all the company's systems analysts) might be unique. Trying to find and use a comparison group for that part would be less easy and probably unnecessary. While use of several designs might be possible, if you are conducting an evaluation for the first time, you are well advised to keep it neat and simple by selecting one appropriate design.

To help further with your choice of a design, Chapter 3 presents a brief description of each. In addition, the charts on the following pages may help you.

Use Figure 2 if you are planning the evaluation before the program cycle starts or if you are designing an original pilot test or experiment. In these situations, choose the best design you think you will be able to implement. If possible, use the true control group design. If you think you might decide against choosing a great design—one with a true randomized control group—then try for a non-equivalent control group. If you cannot find a non-equivalent control group either, or if you are doubtful about finding a good one, then consider a time-series design. Only choose a single group pre-post design (Design 6) if you have absolutely no other choice.

Use Figure 3 if you are planning the evaluation in the middle of the program cycle during which the program must be evaluated. In this case, you will need to look backwards, first of all, to see how participants were selected for the program. You may have to do some searching of records or questioning of personnel to find out exactly what process was used. If you are told the selection was more or less random, keep questioning to find out what the "less random" part was. For example, perhaps there was random selection except that nurses on the night shift, for scheduling reasons, could not be in the program. In such a case, you could treat your data as though they came from a true control group design. When interpreting results, though, you would have to explain that they pertain only to those who were really part of the random selection—in this case, people who do not work the night shift.

TABLE 1 Evaluation Designs

		WHO IS MEASURED		
		Experimental group only These designs can only answer questions related to the way one program works.	More than one group These designs can answer questions comparing the effects of the program or experiment with some alternative.	
			True Control	Non-equivalent Control
WHAT MEASURES ARE MADE	Pretest and Posttest	Design 6	Design 1	Design 3
	Posttest only	not recommended	Design 2	not recommended
	Time Series	Design 4	good, but unusual	Design 5

Titles of the Six Designs:

Design 1: The True Control Group, Pretest-Posttest Design
Design 2: The True Control Group, Posttest Only Design
Design 3: The Non-Equivalent Control Group, Pretest-Posttest Design
Design 4: The Single Group Time Series Design
Design 5: The Time Series Design with a Non-Equivalent Control Group
Design 6: The Before-and-After Design

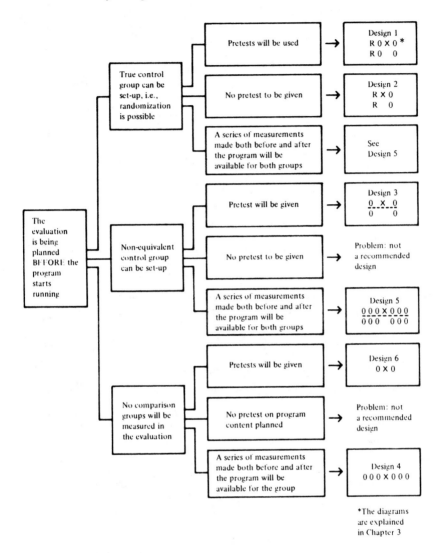

Figure 2. Selecting a design before the program or experiment has started

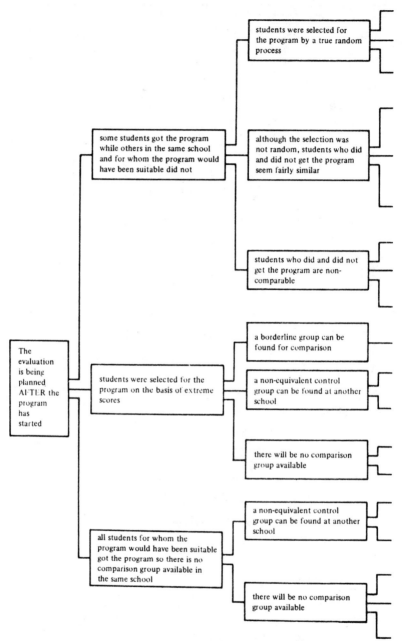

Figure 3. Selecting a design in mid-program. For the sake of clarity, the text discusses *students*. If your evaluation is large-scaled, and will be concerned with *classrooms*, *schools*, or even *districts*, then substitute the proper term when reading the boxes at the first two decision levels. Read, for instance, "some *schools* got the program while others in the same *district* and for whom the program would have been suitable did not" in the

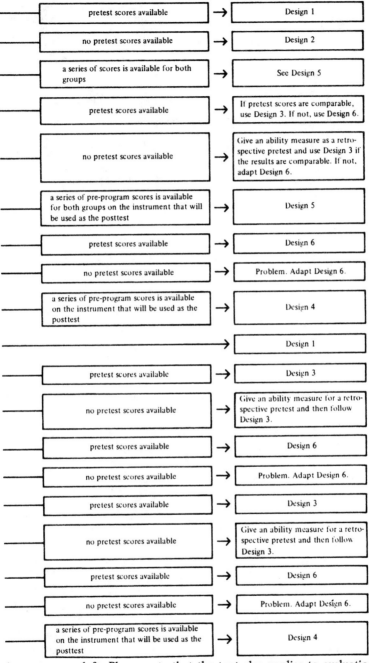

pretest scores available	→	Design 1
no pretest scores available	→	Design 2
a series of scores is available for both groups	→	See Design 5
pretest scores available	→	If pretest scores are comparable, use Design 3. If not, use Design 6.
no pretest scores available	→	Give an ability measure as a retrospective pretest and use Design 3 if the results are comparable. If not, adapt Design 6.
a series of pre-program scores is available for both groups on the instrument that will be used as the posttest	→	Design 5
pretest scores available	→	Design 6
no pretest scores available	→	Problem. Adapt Design 6.
a series of pre-program scores is available on the instrument that will be used as the posttest	→	Design 4
	→	Design 1
pretest scores available	→	Design 3
no pretest scores available	→	Give an ability measure for a retrospective pretest and then follow Design 3.
pretest scores available	→	Design 6
no pretest scores available	→	Problem. Adapt Design 6.
pretest scores available	→	Design 3
no pretest scores available	→	Give an ability measure for a retrospective pretest and then follow Design 3.
pretest scores available	→	Design 6
no pretest scores available	→	Problem. Adapt Design 6.
a series of pre-program scores is available on the instrument that will be used as the posttest	→	Design 4

box at upper left. Please note that the text also applies to evaluation of programs outside education, in which case "students" might actually be employees, clients, consumers, or others. Likewise, large-scaled business evaluations may involve departments, divisions, work sites or branch offices, and so forth.

NOTES

1. Say 25 students or more per group if the students were quite heterogeneous, with a large range of ability or other relevant characteristics; 15 per group if students were a rather homogeneous group to begin with.

2. Criterion-referenced tests (CRT's) compare student scores with predetermined criteria which someone has set up to indicate mastery of subject-matter. Usually these tests are based on objectives that describe specific skills. A student who passes a CRT can be said, with some degree of certainty, to *have* the skills in question. A standardized or norm-referenced test (NRT) on the other hand, compares student scores with those of other students to determine the student's ranking in knowledge about a general subject matter area. From a score on an NRT, it is difficult to tell exactly what part of the subject matter the student actually has mastered.

Chapter 3

Designs—An Overview

Possibly while reading Chapter 2 you came to a decision about what groups you will set up and measure, and at what times you will collect data. You were then able to select from Table 1 the design you were interested in implementing. If this was the case, you will probably now just want to read the brief description in this chapter of the design that you selected and then turn right away to the pages in Chapters 4, 5, or 6 where the design is dealt with in detail. However, if you have not yet selected a design, you should read the brief descriptions of the six designs in this chapter.

Remember that you might select different designs for different instruments.

The Notation Used for Diagramming Each Design

The simple notation employed in the classic work by Campbell and Stanley (1966) is used throughout this book to diagram the various designs. The diagrams use the following symbols:

"R"   means random assignment

"------"   drawn horizontally, separating the two groups, indicates that the groups were not randomly assigned, that is, the groups are non-equivalent

"O"   indicates a measurement of some kind, an Observation

"X"   indicates the program to be evaluated; the eXperimental program, or, in the case of a short experiment, the treatment given to the experimental group

The diagrams all follow this format:

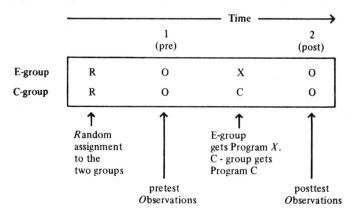

This notation is used in the following presentation of six designs. These are the same six designs as those filling the cells of Table 1 on page 47. Note that the diagrams which follow omit the "C" representing the program received by the control group while the experimental group is receiving Program X. This is done in order to keep the diagram as clear and uncluttered as possible. It must always be remembered though, that *it is not necessary for the control group to get no program.* Indeed, the control group should ideally receive a competing program, the alternative against which Program X is to be compared.

The remainder of this chapter diagrams and describes each of the six designs.

Design 1: The True Control Group, Pretest-Posttest Design

	Time	
	1 (pre)	2 (post)
Experimental Group	R O	X O
Control Group	R O	O

This is the classical true experiment. Persons for whom Program X would be appropriate are *randomly* assigned to form two groups, one which *will* get Program X and one group which will *not*. The group which does not get Program X may get no program at all or may get an alternative program (Program C). The pretest scores can be used to check that the groups started out as more or less equivalent. If at the end of the program, the mean posttest score for the E-group is significantly higher than the mean posttest score for the C-group, this difference can be attributed to the effect of Program X as opposed to the effect of the alternative program. This is a very good design; it permits a powerful test to be made between Program X and the alternative.

Design 2: The True Control Group, Posttest Only Design

	Time		
	1 (pre)		2 (post)
Experimental Group	R	X	O
Control Group	R		O

This is also a "true experimental design." It is exactly like Design 1 *except that no pretest is used*. This design is useful when a pretest might interfere with the program effects in some way or when a pretest is not available or would take too much time. The random assignment of students to either the E-group or the C-group will generally have ensured equivalent groups. This design is often employed when the measurements to be made are measurements of attitudes.

Note that because of the random assignment which should have equated the groups on most variables (especially if numbers in the groups were large enough—say 20 or more), it is possible in this design to wait until the end of a program before deciding exactly what the posttest will be. Equally, tests can be added which had not originally been planned. Design 2 can be easily used in conjunction with Design 1. You might pre- and posttest achievement, for example, but assess attitudes using a posttest only.

Design 3: The Non-Equivalent Control Group, Pretest-Posttest Design

	Time	
	1 (pre)	2 (post)
Experimental Group	O X	O
Control Group	O	O

This pretest-posttest design with a non-equivalent (non-randomized) control group is like Design 1 except that the control group was *not* formed by random assignment. To emphasize the fact that the control group is non-equivalent (non-randomized), the diagram has a dotted line separating the E- and C-groups. This is a very useful design for evaluation in the schools. The pretest scores permit a check on the similarity of the two groups—their similarity, at least, with respect to the measurement used.

This design can be used when you cannot randomly assign students to programs, but must work with intact classrooms. Some classes which are not getting the experimental program can form a non-equivalent control group for the classes which are in the experimental program.

If enough classrooms are available, you might check whether classes rather than students can be randomly assigned, yielding the more powerful Design 1.

Design 4: The Single Group Time Series Design

	Time					
	1	2	3	4	5	6
Experimental Group	O	O	O X	O	O	O

This design uses the persons in the program as their own control group. The *same measurement* is made on the *same group of people* at *regular intervals* several times before and several times after the program. By seeing if Program X appears to disturb the trend in the results, you can assess whether or not Program X might have had an impact on the outcome measure. This design, like the before-and-after design, only requires measurements on one group, but it is a vast improvement over the before-and-after design. Exactly how a time-series design permits better interpretation of results than does the before-and-after design can be illustrated by considering the following situations. Suppose a pretest-posttest design showed a five-month gain in reading:

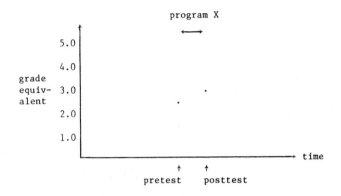

Now suppose the time series measures were added to the same graph and then the graph looked like this:

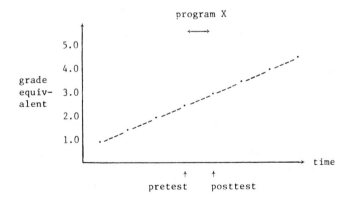

It appears that scores had been rising before the program and they simply continued to rise at the same rate. The program did not appear to do any harm, but also did not seem to change anything for the better.

Now, suppose that the time series measures added to the same initial diagram had made it look like this:

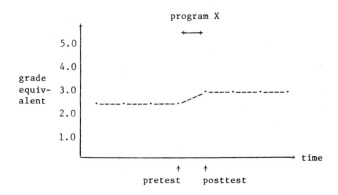

This time interpretation of the same pre-post gain is quite different. The program appears to have caused an upward jump in reading scores and produced the only large gain recorded during the time series measurements.

As you can see, the great advantage of a time series design over a single group pre-post design comes from obtaining a *series* of measurements before and after the implementation of a program. This gives you a more accurate picture of the effect that the program has had than when you have only one measure before and one measure after the program.

The main problem with the time series design is this: Even if you note a clear change in the observations following the implementation of Program X, it is difficult to know for certain whether X caused the change or whether X just happened to occur at about the time that the measures would have changed anyway, because of some other events. However, you can frequently rule out such coincidences.

A time series design is an excellent way to *monitor program performance* for formative, on-going evaluation. Whether the repeated observations are standardized tests, criterion-referenced tests or questionnaires—as long as the test is kept the same—a plot of scores can provide a clear picture of progress over an extended time period.

Two Kinds of Time Series Designs

The time series design comes in two varieties. One involves measurements on the same group of people. This can be called the *longitudinal type* of time series design to distinguish it from the other, more common one, the *successive groups* type. In a successive groups type of time series design, the same *category* of people is measured each time rather than the same *actual* people. For example, instead of measuring and plotting reading scores for the same students as they move from first to second to third grade (a longitudinal time series), you might measure and plot the scores of the first grade students each year for several years. In this case, successive groups are measured. Please notice that in a successive groups time series it might be difficult to tell if changes that are noticed are due to the nature of the particular group of students or to the nature of the program the students receive.

Both kinds of time series designs, longitudinal and successive groups, are discussed in more detail in Chapter 5.

Design 5: The Time Series with a
Non-Equivalent Control Group

	Time					
	1	2	3	4	5	6
Experimental Group	O	O	O	X	O	O	O
Non-equivalent Control Group	O	O	O		O	O	O

This design is exactly like Design 4, but with the addition of a non-equivalent control group. *Two* groups of people are measured regularly before the program and then one group gets Program X, but the other does not; the other might get an alternative program or no program.

The addition of a comparison group to Design 4 makes for a much stronger design. If some external, unrelated, event just happened to coincide with Program X, its effects should show up in the C-group as well as in the E-group. Thus, this particular alternative explanation for the results can often be ruled out when there is a non-equivalent control group. Furthermore, as indicated by the dotted box ( ), this design incorporates the pre-post, non-equivalent control group design (Design 3) and so can give you all the information which that design gives you, plus more. If you are planning to use Design 5, read about Designs 3 and 4 as well.

Design 6: The Before-and-After Design

	Time	
	1 (pre)	2 (post)
Experimental Group	O X	O

One group of people takes a pretest, gets Program X, and then takes a posttest. The results might be compared with "reference" or "norm" groups or with what was expected or hoped for. Considerable problems occur when trying to establish any judgments about Program X on the basis of this design. However, Chapter 6 of this book contains various suggestions for making the most of this design, a design which continues to be common in evaluation, even in summative evaluations.

Major Threats to the Implementation of Designs

Selecting a design is one thing; getting it accurately installed and flawlessly working is another. Even if you are able to establish a randomized, true control group or a non-equivalent control group, there are still potential problems in the actual implementation of the design:

1. *Differences between E- and C-groups in time spent on the program.* A factor which is increasingly recognized as affecting student achievement in a subject is the time spent on that subject by the student. A program that provides lengthy instruction may turn out better results among students no matter what the comparative quality of that instruction. In analyzing program results, therefore, you may want to take into account the time allocated per day to the program and also the attendance records of students. You may even decide to compare an E-group's results with the C-group's results only for those students who were exposed to instruction for the same amount of time.

2. *Attrition.* People drop out of programs and control groups for many reasons: absence from school or work, for illness, transfers to a different classroom or department, moving out of the area, and so on. The loss of data from those people sometimes will affect program results. If slower students or less motivated employees drop out of a new program, for example, the new program will obtain higher average

scores simply because of this loss of certain participants. The loss of people from the groups originally selected to be the E- and C-groups is called "attrition," "mortality," or *loss of cases* in the literature on designs.

3. *The problem of confounds.* In a two-group design, such as Designs 1, 2, and 3, a confound is *something extraneous to the program which happens to one group* (either the E-group or C-group) *but not to the other group, and which could influence the outcome measures for the program.* If the C-group got out of school every day a half hour earlier than the E-group, this fact alone could cause student attitudes to be more favorable toward the C-group's program. With a one-group design, such as Designs 4 and 6, a confound is an extraneous event which occurs at the same time as the program and might be expected to influence the program's outcome measures. For example, if in a time series design the group under study got a new supervisor on or around the same day they began to use the new program, then it would be next to impossible to know whether it was the new supervisor who caused any detected changes or whether it was the new program.

Large numbers of experimental units (students, classrooms, employees, teams) provide some protection against confounds. If you are working with 20 classrooms it isn't likely that all 20 will get new teachers just when they get the new program. In general, when comparing E-groups with C-groups consisting of many cases, differences in what happens to them, apart from the program itself, will tend to average out, sometimes favoring the E-group, sometimes the C-group.

4. *The problem of contamination.* Contamination occurs when the methods or materials of a new program which the E-group is receiving are used, to some extent, by the supposed control group or vice versa. For example, the E-group teacher may share films with his or her friend who is teaching the C-group. Or, over discussions in the lunch room, the best ideas and methods from the E-group may be picked up by the C-group foreman. Obviously the problem of avoiding contamination is most acute when E- and C-groups are at the same site.

One protection against Program X's leaking over into the control group is to discuss the problem with the staff involved. Explain the difficulty of evaluating the new program if you are not able to isolate it, and then ask for their suggestions and cooperation. Contamination may be less of a problem when E- and C-groups are at different sites and/or when the C-group is also receiving a new program so that the teachers or other group supervisors are sufficiently involved with their own new methods and materials and are not likely to be picking up the E-group's methods and materials.

The four problems just discussed—differential program time, attrition, confounds, and contamination—are all problems to which you must attend when you attempt to *interpret* the results you have obtained.

For Further Reading

Campbell, D. T., & Stanley, J. C. (1966). *Experimental and quasi-experimental designs for research.* Chicago: Rand McNally.

Dayton, C. M. (1970). *Design of educational experiments.* New York: McGraw-Hill.

Edwards, A. L. (1972). *Experimental design in psychological research.* New York: Holt, Rinehart & Winston.

Isaac, S., & Michael, W. B. (1971). *Handbook in research and evaluation.* San Diego: Robert R. Knapp.

Chapter 4

Designs 1, 2, and 3:
The Control Group Designs

In this chapter, Designs 1, 2, and 3 are each described in detail. If you turn to the design you have decided to use, you will find a flowchart showing the essential steps in the implementation of the design (these steps may look deceptively simple!). Each design is also accompanied by a few examples. A discussion of the analysis and presentation of data for the design follows the examples.

Design 1:
The True Control Group,
Pretest-Posttest Design

Diagram

	Time			
	1 (pre)			2 (post)
Experimental Group	R	O	X	O
Control Group	R	O		O

Summary

Two equivalent groups are formed by random assignment. In education, the units which are randomly assigned might be students, classrooms, or schools depending on the number of each available to you and at which level the program is supposed to show its greatest impact.[1] In the work place, units might be employees, teams, departments, sites, and so on. The two groups are measured both before the program or experimental treatment starts (the pretest) and after it has had time to produce an effect (the posttest).

The Essential Steps in Implementing Design 1

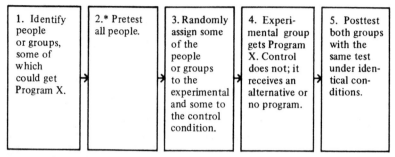

1. Identify people or groups, some of which could get Program X.	2.* Pretest all people.	3. Randomly assign some of the people or groups to the experimental and some to the control condition.	4. Experimental group gets Program X. Control does not; it receives an alternative or no program.	5. Posttest both groups with the same test under identical conditions.

*Steps 2 and 3 might occur in the reverse order, which would then match the diagram which shows "R"–randomizing–occurring prior to the pretest (i.e., prior to time 1). Randomization has to *follow* the pretest if *blocking* on the pretest–explained on page 150 is employed.

Examples of Design 1 in Use

The reading machine example. A school purchased a machine designed to assist students in learning to read. Some materials for the machine were also purchased, but since they represented a significant slice of the school's available monies, there was a need to know how effective the reading machine materials were. In order to assess this, the staff decided to do some formative evaluation by means of a short experiment following Design 1. A test was built to assess the results of three weeks' daily work on the materials already purchased for the machine. Students for whom this work was appropriate were selected and randomly divided into two groups. The students in one group (the experimental group) worked on the reading machine each day for three weeks whereas students in the other group (the control group) simply continued with their regular reading program. The regular program was modified, however, to teach the same vocabulary as was taught by the reading machine. At the end of three weeks, students were tested to see if the reading machine group (experimental group) had learned more than the control group.

The management-by-objectives system example. A suggestion had been made that the school board of a large urban district should purchase and implement a commercially developed management-by-objectives (MBO) system for junior high school math programs. Unwilling to undertake such expense without evidence of the effectiveness of the system, the district asked for a limited tryout and an evaluation. The board emphasized that schools should not be required to participate in this tryout.

The research staff requested that junior high schools indicate whether or not they would participate in the MBO system were it made available to them. From the schools that volunteered to try out the system, the research staff chose four high, four medium, and four low achieving schools on the basis of last year's test results and then randomly selected two schools at each achievement level to become the experimental and control groups. Pretests were given in all 12 schools selected in this manner. The MBO system was then made available to the six schools in the experimental group. At the end of one year, a posttest on math achievement was given in all 12 schools. In their report to the board, the research staff was able to give strong evidence regarding the impact which the MBO system had had on achievement. They emphasized that their conclusions were strictly applicable only to schools volunteering to accept the system, and the results, which were positive, might be different if the system were imposed rather than requested. The board commended the staff on the thoroughness and clarity of its study.

An employee service example. A large bank concerned with morale and turnover decided to try offering a child care referral service for its employees as a way to encourage trained employees to remain with the bank. Since this type of employee program was one the bank was unfamiliar with managing, it decided to try out the program before implementing it in all branches. Data on turnover rates and costs and on morale were collected prior to program implementation. Then 15 branches were randomly selected to have a special child care referral office open on site two days a week for a six-month period. The remaining 15 branches continued as usual without the program. At the end of 6 months, turnover rates and costs and a measure of morale were compared, and, indeed, those branches with the referral program had significantly lower turnover rates and higher morale. The bank concluded by expanding the program to all its branches and decided to use the referral service to collect additional data on child care problems to ascertain whether other types of child care assistance might be of mutual benefit to the bank and its employees.

Presentation and Analysis of Data for Design 1

The great virtue of this design is that, when it has been properly implemented, you will be able to draw strong conclusions about the effect of Program X on posttest scores. Furthermore, it allows you to detect even small, short-term improvements; that is, it can be a *sensitive* test of a program.

Two kinds of information should be reported in order to do justice to Design 1: implementation data about the design and outcome data.

Reporting about implementation of the design

Showing how successfully the design was implemented will involve considering the following questions:

1. *Program implementation.* Did the E-group receive the program? This question will be answered in the section of your report where you describe what the program looked like in operation.

2. *Contamination.* Did the C-group *not* get the program or any piece of it? That is, was contamination avoided? This requires at least some documentation of what happened in the C-group.

3. *Confounds.* Were confounds avoided? Can you assure that there were no consistent differences between what happened to the E-group and C-group other than Program X, differences which might reasonably be expected to either raise or lower scores on the outcome measures?

4. *Attrition.* Was there any difference between the *number* of "cases" lost from the E-group and number of cases lost from the C-group? Was there any difference in the *kinds* of cases (students, classrooms, or schools) which had to be dropped from the analysis in each group? Include a table in your report such as the one shown below to summarize attrition.[2]

TABLE 2
Number of Students Dropped
From the Analysis for Various Reasons

Reason	Number dropped from E-group	Number dropped from C-group
Absent for posttest		
Absent from school during the program		
Removed from group at request of parent		
Left the school		
Other reasons		
Total number dropped		

Because the E-group and C-group may be different sizes, it would be advisable to put in parentheses the percentage of the pretest group size which is represented by the "number dropped" figure. For example, if an E-group consisted of 300 students for whom there were pretest results, and 30 were dropped from the analysis because they were absent from school for more than a specified number of days during the program, then in the second row the entry in the E-group column should be "30 (10%)." This shows that 30 students were dropped, which represents 10% of the original E-group (30/300 × 100 = 10%). If the dropout rates for the E- and C-groups were very different, try to explain them. Make inquiries; try to find out what happened. If you suspect that *students with certain characteristics* dropped out of the program, you might tabulate appropriate data and examine it. A good way to generate reasonable hypotheses about what might cause attrition is to interview a random sample of employees who have dropped out of each group.

Example. A marketing training coordinator suggested to the formative evaluator that more lower ability employees had dropped out of a training program than higher ability employees. He noted that 12 low ability and only 8 high ability employees had dropped. The evaluator collected this data:

	Dropouts		Total
	low ability	high ability	
E-group	12 (60%)	8 (40%)	20
C-group	10 (59%)	7 (41%)	17
Total	22	15	37

The evaluator pointed out that although it was true that more low ability employees than high ability employees had dropped out of the E-group, the same situation applied to the C-group too. Since the percentage of people dropping out was very similar in both E- and C-groups, attrition would probably not affect the relative performance of the two programs when outcomes were compared.

Analyzing, reporting, and discussing mean outcomes from Design 1

Tables and graphs. Below is a simple table for reporting the results from Design 1, the True Control Group, Pretest-Posttest Design.

TABLE 3

Pre- and Posttest Results
for the Experimental and Control Groups

	N	Pretest			Posttest		
		Mean	SD	t-test of difference	Mean	SD	t-test of difference
E-group							
C-group							

N is the number kept for analysis; it equals the number of cases for which there were pretest results minus the total number dropped from the analysis. The column labeled Mean contains scores for each group on each test. The standard deviation (SD) related to each mean is reported in the adjacent column. The t-test of difference is a test of the significance of the difference between the mean scores for the experimental and control groups on the pretest or posttest. If you used either simple or "blocked" randomization (see page 150) to form the groups, the appropriate t-test to be used is the t-test for unmatched groups, sometimes called the noncorrelated t-test. If you used a matching method (page 154), then use the t-test for matched groups.

Example

TABLE N
Pretest and Posttest Results
for Tutors and Non-Tutors

	N	Pretest (ability)			Posttest (Arithmetic)		
		Mean	SD	t-test of diff.	Mean	SD	t-test of diff.
tutors	8	24.00	7.25	0.25	30.30	5.10	4.16*
non-tutors	14	24.86	7.12		15.80	8.60	

*statistically significant at the .05 level

The example illustrates the way Design 1 results are interpreted. The t-test for pretest scores was not significant, and this is indicated by *lack of* an asterisk. This means that on the pretest, the two groups were more or less equivalent. Randomization was successful; any difference between the means was no more than one would expect due to chance. Having established that the groups were equivalent to begin with, one then looks at results after the program and compares the two group means again by using a t-test. For the example shown, there is a large difference between the posttest means; and not surprisingly the t-test shows it to be significant, that is, bigger than could have been expected to occur by chance. For the example shown, the evaluator will write in her report:

As was expected because of the use of random selection, the tutors and non-tutors were initially
equivalent on the ability measure used as the pretest. After the program, however, the mean posttest
score of the tutors was significantly higher than
the non-tutors' mean score. This gain by tutors can

be attributed to their participation in the tutoring program.

In addition to the table, results from Design 1 can be displayed graphically. Graphic representation is highly recommended because graphs are quickly understood and interpreted. In addition, graphs are almost always preferable when presenting results to a live audience.

If the pre- and posttests were the *same test* (or an equivalent or parallel form), then this graph will always be appropriate:

Example

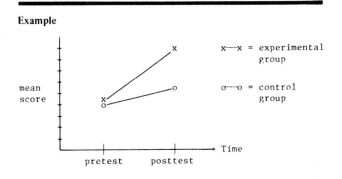

Figure Q.   Mean scores of the E-group and C-group
            on the pretest and posttest

If the pretest was *different* from the posttest—an ability test perhaps—display only the posttest scores. This is the simplest method of display and is perfectly acceptable if there was no significant difference between pretest scores:

Example

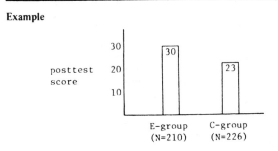

Figure R.   Mean posttest scores of the
            E-group and C-group

Comparing pretest scores. If you have randomized a fairly large number of people or classrooms prior to the pretest, mean pretest scores between groups should show *no* significant difference. No significant difference in pretest scores indicates, as one would expect, that chance has produced two groups more or less equivalent in achievement. The chance of this equivalence happening is greater, of course, if some form of blocking, matching, or stratification (page 162) occurred prior to randomized assignment.

If the t-test for the significance of the difference between the two pretest means is non-significant, then no further attention to the pretest is necessary. Your interpretation at the end of the whole study can rest solely on the posttest means.

If, on the other hand, pretest means *are* significantly different, you have to face up to this problem. There are several possibilities:

1. Perhaps it is not too late to reassign groups to programs. If you did not block or match according to some available scores in initially forming the groups, do so this time using the pretest scores you have now.
2. Take a close look at the people making up the two groups. Are there "outliers"—extremely high or low scores—that have distorted one of the means? If so, drop these scores from the analysis.
3. If someone other than yourself did the randomizing, check with that person to see if a few "special cases" were in fact *not* randomly assigned and correct this if possible or drop those cases from the analysis.
4. Treat this design as a Non-Equivalent Control Group Design, Design 3.

Comparing posttest scores. If the experimental group's mean posttest score was higher than the control group's mean and the t-test was statistically significant, you can state, for Design 1:

The results showed that the experimental program
produced posttest scores which were significantly
higher than those of the control group.

It is probably better, though, to avoid the terms *experimental* and *control*, and instead describe the groups as occurs here:

The results showed that participation in the biology
lab program produced posttest scores which were significantly higher than those of the students who
participated in the regular lecture-based biology
course and received no lab experience.

Please note the crucial question in interpreting results from Design 1:

Was the posttest *mean* for one group significantly different from the posttest *mean* for the other group?

It is *not* good procedure to test the difference between the *gains* from pretest to posttest for both groups. Comparing gains usually penalizes the group whose pretest score was higher. How can you know whether a gain of X points from the higher score represents the same amount of growth as a gain of X points from the lower? Maybe the going gets rougher after a certain level of achievement has been attained. Or perhaps the reverse is true. Maybe mastering the basics is difficult, and once a certain minimal score is attained, gains are easy. Since you cannot know whether one or neither of these is the case, compare the *same tests* between the two groups, NOT the differences in score gains from pretest to posttest.

```
R    O    X    O ⤷  ⟵  This is the comparison
R    O         O ⤴      which must be made.
```

When deciding whether to take differences in mean posttest scores seriously, the presentation of *confidence limits* is often more useful than a t-test. Confidence limits assist, as well, in interpretation of educational significance. While a test of significance tells you whether the difference you have found between scores is big *enough* to transcend chance, confidence limits give you an estimate of the *range* of differences you would obtain between the E- and C-groups were you to repeat the study again and again. This range not only gives you an idea of how big the *actual* difference between the groups might be; it also enables a quick check on whether the difference obtained is significant. A significant difference, if you think about it, will *not* include *zero* within the range of its confidence limits.

If the E-group's mean posttest score is *higher* than the control group's mean, but not *significantly* different, you might have a data analyst try a more powerful statistical test such as the analysis of variance (ANOVA), described in Chapter 7, or analysis of covariance (ANCOVA), discussed in most basic statistics texts but of controversial value. On the other hand, you might just note:

The mean posttest score of the participants in Program X was higher than the mean for those in Program C, but the difference could have been due to chance variation. That is, the difference was not large enough to be labeled statistically significant.

If the experimental group's mean posttest score was significantly *lower* than the control group's, then the experimental program has not produced better results. This suggests that the experimental program had a negative effect on the outcome measure.

What to do with results other than means

The table, graph, and analysis for Design 1 described above focused on measurement where the E- and C-groups each yield a *mean* score for comparison. This will not always, of course, be the case. Another summary statistic for outcome measures might be, for instance, the percentage or proportion of respondents answering or performing a certain way. The table and graph formats described here, however, can be adapted for use in any instance where the outcomes of the E- and C-groups can be expressed as a *single number,* though the exact statistical tests to be performed will differ in some cases.

A more difficult data analysis problem occurs when the outcome measure for the E- and C-groups is an *objectives-based test.* Results from these tests are not easily crunched into a single number for comparison. Each group's performance is usually expressed as an average or mastery count *per objective.* If the test has been based on many objectives, how are you going to compare outcomes? There are several alternatives, and probably the clearest way to present the data will be to use more than one:

1. *Find a single mean or proportion for each group that seems to ade-quately represent group performance,* and use the table, graph, and statistical analyses outlined in the last section. This statistic might be, for instance, the mean percentage of objectives mastered per class, or the proportion of students within a class passing some critical set or number of objectives. If scores per objective are available, you might also report the average score over several objectives per group. Which of these numbers most clearly represents performance will depend on the questions your evaluation must answer. One thing is clear: if you have gone to the trouble of administering objectives-based tests, you have assembled much richer information than can be represented by a single number. Besides, reporting only differences in numbers of students passing or number of objectives mastered leaves critical questions un-answered:

   • Were the objectives mastered trivial ones, or were they important? Maybe one of the groups mastered a lot of less crucial objectives, while the other emphasized the important ones.
   • Were all the objectives equally easy to pass or were some "real buggers"? Perhaps one of the programs pulled students through a few objectives which were difficult to teach or for which stringent passing criteria had been set.

2. *Augment or replace your single number analyses with more detailed depictions of program results.* A useful adjustment which still yields a single statistic per group is to segregate the objectives by difficulty or importance, or both, and then report results according to these classifications. Before outcome data are in, have members of the staff or evaluation audience rank order the objectives or prepare an objectives hierarchy to identify those representing critical skills (methods for ranking objectives and assembling hierarchies are detailed in Morris & Fitz-Gibbon, 1978a). Then compute average or percentage of mastery for these smaller groups of similar objectives. The extreme of this procedure would be to identify *single* most critical objectives and compare the proportion of students passing each of these.

3. *Prepare graphs and tables to summarize the findings per objective.* Graphs, in particular, will display enough of your complex data to allow the evaluation audience to draw comparisons of its own. "It is sometimes said," write Glass and Stanley in their classic text on data analysis, "that the facts speak for themselves. In reality, statistics often stand speechless and silent, tables are sometimes tongue-tied, and only the graph cries aloud its message" (Glass & Stanley, 1970, p. 42).

Bar graphs are particularly useful in presenting data about the achievement of objectives, each bar representing one objective. From a glance at a bar graph, the strengths and weaknesses of programs can be quickly seen. In the sample shown below, the posttest results for two math programs, X and C, are displayed with objectives grouped together.

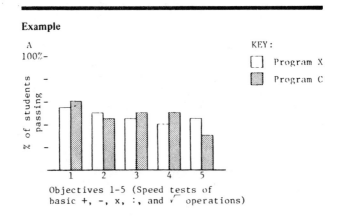

Example

KEY:

☐ Program X

▨ Program C

Objectives 1-5 (Speed tests of basic +, -, x, :, and √ operations)

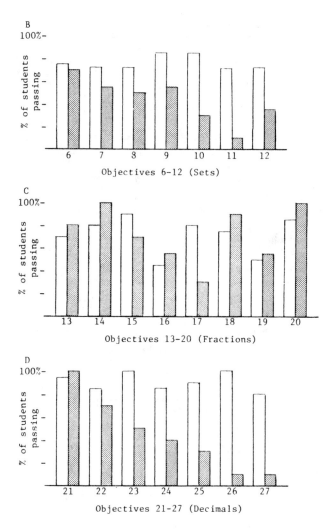

Figure W.   Posttest results for four
groups of objectives

You will notice that in order to avoid cluttering up the figures with numbers, only lines are drawn to indicate the 20%, 40%, 60%, 80%, and 100% passing rates. The passing rates for the speed tests (A) were generally below 60%, and the two programs did not appear to differ. If you wished to see if either program produced *better* speed tests, you could *sum* the scores for objectives 1 to 5 and compute a mean for each program. You could then apply a t-test to see if the difference between the means was statistically significant. It appears that Program X was more successful at teaching sets (group B) and considerably more successful at teaching decimals (group D). Looking at group D, you might infer that perhaps the Program C students never reached the last five objectives in decimals. Program C appears to have produced better results with fractions (group C); perhaps it spent more time on their instruction.

Most texts on the subject of attitude and achievement measurement describe more detailed methods for data presentation than will fit here (see Henerson, Morris, & Fitz-Gibbon, 1978; Morris & Fitz-Gibbon, 1978b). One further suggestion, however: When displaying differences between E- and C-groups for attitude instruments, consider using a line graph to portray results. A questionnaire scored item-by-item represents, after all, an objectives-based instrument where each question measures achievement of an attitude.

Example. Data display showing mean response of E- and C-groups to an end-of-program employee attitude questionnaire:

	1 excel-lent	2 good	3 average	4 below average	5 poor
1. How do you rate your department's salary record?	1	2	3	4	5
2. How satisfied are you with your job progress?	1	2	3	4	5
3. How secure do you feel in your job?	1	2	3	4	5
4. How well does your supervisor motivate you?	1	2	3	4	5
5. What kind of job does management do in running this company?	1	2	3	4	5
6. How adequate are the communications in your department?	1	2	3	4	5

↑ C-group average response   ↑ E-group average response

This graph was constructed by first computing the mean response to each question for each group. These averages were then located on a copy of the questionnaire itself and included in the evaluation report.

The graph seems to show little difference in the response of E- and C-groups except that the C-group tends to feel the communications in its department are quite good whereas the E-group does not. To determine whether the size of the difference between E- and C-group responses on item 6 was statistically significant, apply a t-test.

The intent of these suggestions has been to help you enrich data presentation for a control group design where objectives-based outcome measures have been used. As a footnote, consider a word of caution about *objectives-based achievement tests:* The test performance data you present depict *mastery* of objectives. Such information is useful only where standards of mastery are realistic. Should you report such information, it will be your responsibility to describe what mastery means.

Summary of analysis, reporting, and discussion for Design 1

In reporting the results of a true control group, pretest-posttest design, discuss first the extent to which the design was adequately implemented, the loss of cases, and any possible confounds and contamination. If none of these threats, or any others you can think of, seem to present insurmountable problems to interpretation of the results, then present the results. If objectives-based tests or attitude instruments were used, you might have to report results in narrative or graphic form. The principal Design 1 questions will remain the same, however, no matter what instruments you have used: Were the groups equivalent on the pretest, and, if so, was there then a statistically significant difference between posttest scores? If statistically significant differences have been found, you will then need to examine the educational significance of the results.

The Practical or Educational Significance of Program Effects

Even if you have found that the experimental group produced a significantly higher mean score than the control group or if the confidence limits of the difference you found do not include zero, you will still need to decide the *practical* or *educational* significance of the gain from the program: How *valuable* is the difference?

Statistical significance, after all, only tells you whether or not you are safe in drawing certain conclusions about an experiment. If you can say that on the posttest the E-group did better then the C-group at a .05 significance level, this means that if, in fact, there was no real difference between the two groups after the program, the particular difference *you* found would only occur five times out of a hundred. This small chance makes you feel safe in putting forth the idea that there is a real difference between the groups. The statistical significance assures you that the result probably wasn't due to chance variation. Given the number of cases you had, and the variability you found in the scores, the difference you found was too large to be due to chance.

However, statistical significance does not tell you anything about how *valuable* the difference was. For one thing, *statistical* significance is heavily dependent on the number of people or classes in your groups. A program which taught a large number of E-group students, say 300, to answer correctly two more items than the control group could answer might show a statistically significant superiority. But is learning two more facts in the course of a year *educationally* significant? And if the program cost more, was it worth it?

Obviously you'll need some way to get a handle on the practical significance of a program. To aid this discussion, the word *effect* will be restricted to represent the *difference in posttest means* between the groups that did and did not get the program. Thus, if the results on the posttests were

mean for E-group = 30

mean for C-group = 26

then the effect of the program was 4 points in favor of the E-group.

There are several ways to assess the practical or educational significance of program effects. None of them is easy. All of them require rummaging around to take a closer look at the people themselves, the tests used, and people's expectations. You'll need to know, perhaps, who benefited in what ways, and you may even have to define what "benefited" means. From the suggestions that follow, pick out one or more that makes sense to you. Most of this discussion assumes the posttest results under consideration are achievement tests.

1. *Use teacher judgment as a criterion reference.* Whether the test was a standardized test or an in-house developed test, have a few teachers or experts who know the particular grade level and subject area study the test in detail and, before they have seen the test results, check off

   • items no one should have missed
   • items the average person would be expected to get correct in the time which was available
   • items only the best participants would be expected to answer correctly

   From this information, a range of scores can be drawn up which represents *experts' judgment* of the test content and predictions for reasonable achievement. The obtained results can be compared with these judgments. Ask yourself, "Which items accounted for the differences between groups? The easy ones? Or did either group seem to do better with the more difficult material?"

2. *Try an ability reference.* Compare the effects of the program upon students of different abilities. On the posttest, what was the range in scores between the slowest students and the brightest students? Was it broad or narrow? Did one group seem to benefit particularly? How do the effects due to the program compare with the effects you can attribute to ability?

3. *Norm-reference the effects.* If you used a standardized test, compare the effect of the program with national norms. Did raw score differences, for instance, represent a difference of one-half a month or six months' grade equivalent scores?

4. *Perform an item analysis.* For each item, calculate the *percentage* of the E-group and C-group who passed, and try to locate the items which made the most difference. Perhaps the significant difference was due mainly to items dealing with just one content area and otherwise there was no difference between the groups. If so, you'll have to ask people how important that particular content area was. On the other hand, if the experimental program shows more people passing almost every item, then it appears that the experimental program was successful across many kinds of content.

Design 2:
The True Control Group,
Posttest Only Design

Diagram

	Time	
	1 (pre)	2 (post)
Experimental Group	R X	O
Control Group	R	O

Summary

Two equivalent groups of students, classrooms, teams, or schools[3] are formed by random assignment. One gets Program X or an experimental treatment, and the other does not. Both are measured at the end of the program only.

The Essential Steps in Implementing Design 2

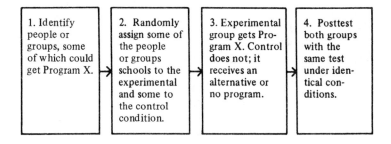

| 1. Identify people or groups, some of which could get Program X. | 2. Randomly assign some of the people or groups schools to the experimental and some to the control condition. | 3. Experimental group gets Program X. Control does not; it receives an alternative or no program. | 4. Posttest both groups with the same test under identical conditions. |

Examples of Design 2 in Use

An early reading program example. Reading specialists in a district wanted to find a method of introducing reading in the first grade which would avoid problems later. They could not be sure whether a strong phonics approach or a strong experimental approach would be best for the students (and parents!) in their particular district. They decided to try both approaches and see which worked best. They put together a series of workshops for each approach and randomly selected ten first-grade teachers for each of these workshops. The teachers were urged to use the methods and materials from the workshops extensively in their classrooms, and regular visits were made to see if this was being done. At the end of the year, a reading posttest was given in all the classrooms.

An example of a short experiment. A team of teachers at a high school planned a human relations program consisting of films, discussions, books, and role-playing, aimed at developing tolerant attitudes toward the values and characteristics of different cultural groups. They randomly assigned the boys to Group X or Group Y and then did the same for the girls. Group X received an introductory unit of the human relations program for three weeks, while Group Y received a new program about careers, a program which also used films, discussions, books, and role-playing. At the end of the three weeks the two groups answered attitude surveys assessing both inter-cultural tolerance and career aspirations. The results for Group X on the human relations questions were compared with the results for Group Y on the human relations questions. Differences were attributed to the program since it could be assumed that the groups had been equivalent to begin with due to random assignment.

Presentation and Analysis of Data for Design 2

There are two basic kinds of information to be reported for Design 2. The first kind of information is data showing how successfully the design was implemented. Second, the results of the outcome measures must be reported for both the E- and C-groups.

Reporting about implementation of the design

Showing how successfully the design was implemented will involve considering the following questions:

1. *The randomization procedure used for forming the E- and C-groups.* Was random assignment adequate to assure initially equal groups? Your randomization method will need to be described in order to eliminate doubts about group inequality and therefore warrant the absence of a pretest.

2. *Program implementation.* Did the E-group receive the program? This question will be answered in the section of your report where you describe what the program looked like in operation.

3. *Contamination.* Did the C-group *not* get the program or any piece of it? That is, was contamination avoided? This requires at least some documentation of what happened in the C-group.

4. *Confounds.* Were confounds avoided? Can you assume that there were no consistent differences between what happened to the E-group and C-group other than Program X, differences which might reasonably be expected to either raise or lower scores on the outcome measures?

5. *Attrition.* Was there any difference between the *number* of "cases" lost from the E-group and number of cases lost from the C-group? Was there any differnece in the *kinds* of cases (e.g., students, classrooms, or schools) which had to be dropped from the analysis in each group? For example, did members of the football team miss too much of the program because they took trips for games? If it was found, for instance, that an interpersonal relationships program was officially but not actually implemented in three of four management training groups, but the focus group training program was well-implemented in all groups, this would need to be reported and interpreted. In this case a table like the one below showing loss of cases at various stages of the implementation should be included in the evaluation.[4]

Example

TABLE T
Managers Remaining After Three Stages
of Program Implementation

	number of managers asked to attend workshops	number of managers who completed all workshops	number of managers who implemented programs satis-factorily
Interpersonal relations program			
Focus group training program			

Analyzing, reporting, and discussing outcomes from Design 2

Tables and graphs. The examples below show a way of displaying posttest scores in table and graph form. The t-test in the table can be one of two types. If randomization was simple or blocked, as described in Chapter 8, then use the t-test for unmatched groups, also called a non-correlated t-test. If a matched randomization method was used, then use a t-test for matched groups. If the t-value is significant, this is usually indicated by an asterisk and the footnote to the table "p <.05" (or if you used a .10 level, "p < .10").

TABLE 4   Posttest Mean Scores

	Posttest			
	N	Mean	SD	t-test
E-group	–	– –	–	– – *
C-group	–	– –	–	

(*p   )

A graph is a useful way of displaying results whenever clarity is more important than decimal figure accuracy.

Example

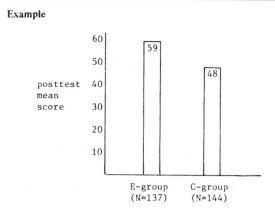

Figure S. Mean scores of the two groups
on the posttest

Interpretation. Your interpretation of results will be identical with that allowed by Design 1. Therefore the discussion on pages 67 to 78 about reporting applies to you as well.

If you find a significant difference between the mean posttest scores as shown by a t-test, you are pretty safe in saying that one program appears more effective than another as long as there have not been any considerable problems with loss of cases, confounds, and contamination. You will emphasize that the random procedure, which you will have described in the section of your report describing the evaluation design, should have ensured equivalent groups to begin with.

As with Design 1, it is sometimes more useful to calculate and present *confidence limits* for the difference between mean scores than to calculate a t-value. Confidence limits give you an estimate of the *range* of differences you would obtain were you to repeat the study again. Your audience can then determine for itself whether such a difference is educationally significant.

If the posttest means were *not* significantly different and you do not think this was due to contamination—to the possibility that the programs themselves were not kept distinct—then you might try an analysis of variance (see Chapter 7) or some "internal" analysis of the data. Perhaps you suspect that the program worked better with some people than others. In the attitude program example above (the one focused on human relations), you might try looking at the mean scores for male and female students separately.

Example. Posttest scores on attitudes

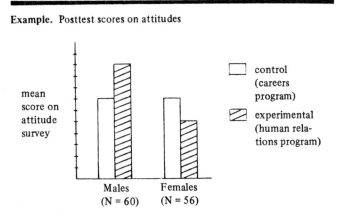

mean
score on
attitude
survey

control
(careers
program)

experimental
(human rela-
tions program)

Males   Females
(N = 60)   (N = 56)

For males, the experimental program appears to have increased positive attitudes; for females, decreased. When these results were averaged, they showed no difference.

You need to remember an important caution about internal analysis. When you start breaking down the groups into smaller sub-groups, results become less stable because of smaller numbers. Tests of significance will check how safe you are in generalizing from these small groups. Furthermore, if you search the data a lot—cut it up in many ways—you vastly increase your chances of finding something "significant" just by chance. The best strategy will be to chop up the data for internal analysis only if you have a good rationale for hypothesizing some differential effects.

Summary of analysis, reporting, and discussion for Design 2

In reporting the results of a true control group, posttest only design, discuss first the extent to which the design was adequately implemented. Because pretest scores are not presented, it will be necessary to describe in detail the randomization procedure that was used to form the groups. A detailed description of the procedure should help to convince the audience that the groups were formed in an unbiased fashion. Also discuss any confounds, contamination, or loss of cases that occurred in the E- and C-groups.

If the design was adequately implemented, present the posttest results and discuss the significance of the difference between E- and C-groups or the actual likely difference as indicated by the confidence limits you have calculated. If *objectives-based tests* or *attitude instruments* were used, you might also have to report results in a more narrative or graphic form, as described on pages 74 to 78. If the differential performance of the two groups was statistically significant, you should consider the educational significance of this difference. *Statistical* significance, after all, only tells you that your results are not likely to have occurred by chance. It does not tell you if your results are of great magnitude, or if they are important enough to influence anybody. You should accompany any report of results, whether for formative or summative evaluation purposes, with an assessment of the *value* of the differences you've uncovered. Pages 78 to 80 discuss this issue in greater detail.

Design 3:
The Non-Equivalent Control Group,
Pretest-Posttest Design

Diagram

	Time	
	1 (pre)	2 (post)
Experimental Group	O X	O
Control Group	O	O

Summary

Two groups which are similar, but which were *not* formed by random assignment, are measured both before and after one of the groups gets the program or the experimental treatment.

The Essential Steps in Implementing Design 3

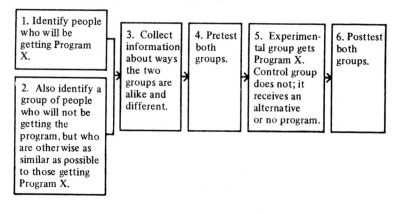

1. Identify people who will be getting Program X.

2. Also identify a group of people who will not be getting the program, but who are otherwise as similar as possible to those getting Program X.

3. Collect information about ways the two groups are alike and different.

4. Pretest both groups.

5. Experimental group gets Program X. Control group does not; it receives an alternative or no program.

6. Posttest both groups.

Examples of Design 3 in Use

A bilingual program example. Fifteen classrooms in one district had received funds for bilingual education programs. The summative evaluator was anxious to measure the extent to which the bilingual programs improved achievement, encouraged more cross-ethnic friendship choices, and improved children's adjustment to school. She realized that she would improve her chances of building a credible case for the effectiveness of the program if she had some kind of control group. Being unable to form a true control group, she looked around for a non-equivalent control group and was able to obtain the cooperation of nine classrooms in a nearby district. These classrooms also contained high percentages of non-English speaking students but did not have bilingual programs. She pretested the fifteen E-group and nine C-group classrooms, observed samples of the classrooms at regular intervals during the school year, and posttested all classrooms at the end of the year.

A junior high math tryout example. A remedial program in mathematics was developed by the Pennsbury Public Schools for junior high students with low competency in basic skills. The program could be costly because of new materials and tutors, and a formative evaluator from the Research and Evaluation Office suggested that the program be tried out for one semester in the four schools in the district's more affluent area which had clamored for its adoption. Since it was a remedial program aimed at basic skills, a basic skills test was given in September, and the lowest 5% of the students were scheduled into the remedial program. Aware that she had erred in using the pretest for selection of an extreme group and would therefore need to rule out *regression* effects, the evaluator foresaw the need for a comparison group. She gave the *same test* in the five other junior high schools in Pennsbury. In each school she identified the students below the cut-off point which had been used in the original schools. At the end of the semester, program participants at all nine schools were given the same test again; this time it was used as the posttest. By comparing the experimental schools' mean with means from the control schools, it was found that posttest scores among experimental program students were greater than those in other programs at the other schools. Since the evaluator had made some effort to control for regression and the effects of students just getting older, differences could be tentatively attributed to the programs.

The evaluation results were open to some challenge, however. For one thing, opponents argued that the program could have succeeded solely because its implementors were volunteers whereas the controls were not. What is more, argued one particularly astute critic, the design doesn't *completely* rule out regression. Since the *program* students were from schools where average math performance was higher, the students selected for the programs were particularly unlucky in obtaining such low pretest scores—more unlucky than their compatriots from the less advantaged control schools. Because of this, the program students would be expected to regress *more* and therefore score deceptively higher on the posttest. The critic was correct, pointing out a common challenge when Design 3 is used with remedial programs.

A preventive medicine example. A nonprofit community health organization had a grant from a foundation to develop and provide a model nutrition education program to senior citizens at a local retirement home as part of a large project on preventive medicine. The organization had to demonstrate that the program was having a significant impact in order to get the project funding renewed for another year. Since all the people in the retirement home were involved in the program, the organization needed to find a non-equivalent control group. Thus, it sought out a similar retirement home in the same city in which the residents were roughly similar to those participating in the nutrition program in terms of variables relating to eating and health problems: foods available at the retirement home, ethnic background, male/female ratio, median age and range, and degree of health problems allowed by the homes on initial acceptance. It was also determined that the residents of the second retirement home had not been given any special education or information about nutrition. Three measures were used with all the seniors both prior to and after the education program for the treatment group: a health screening, a test of nutrition facts, and an eating habits diary.

Presentation and Analysis of Data for Design 3

Design 3 is just like Design 1 except that the groups are not composed by random assignment. The possibility of "non-equivalence" in the control group almost always renders Design 3 less credible than Design 1. You can increase the credibility of a Design 3 study, however, by providing as much information as you can find *that shows the E- and C-groups to be initially alike*. In fact, Design 3 can be rendered nearly as strong as Design 1 if you can show that the two groups are so alike in relevant characteristics that they might as well have been composed randomly. The pretest, which is *required* by this design, serves as a check on *whether the groups are at least comparable on whatever the program intends to change*. Because the pretest is used in this way, it should be a measurement as closely related to the posttest as possible, preferably the same test or an equivalent or parallel form of it.

Even equivalent pretest scores do not always ensure credibility, however. As the Pennsbury math program example above illustrates, you will have problems in interpreting Design 3 results whenever *any* major systematic differences between E- and C-groups can be pinpointed.

Because Design 3 is *more* practically feasible than the true experimental designs, but yields *less* easily interpreted information, it has been discussed extensively of late. Several people have invented variations on the basic design described here, all of them *quasi*-experimental, and some of them worth considering and using. One of these variants (Tallmadge's "Regression Projection Model," described in Horst, Tallmadge, & Wood, 1975; see also Campbell & Stanley, 1966, for an outline of the closely related "Regression-Discontinuity Model") involves regression models and allows the evaluator to use as a non-equivalent control group students who clearly outperform the experimental students on the pretest. Others (Cook & Campbell, 1976) prescribe variation in the sort of program the control group receives and in the types of posttests used. Another (Ball & Bogatz, 1970; see also Cook et al., 1975) has demonstrated a way to control for the effects of cognitive development in young children by comparing performance of the experimental groups' children with a baseline established by measuring a non-equivalent control group composed of children of a particular age. Since these versions of Design 3 demand statistical sophistication or build their credibility on logic more complex than the basic design, they are not elaborated here. If you need or want to know more about designing field research, you should explore these designs further. They may prove useful or inspire your own clever variations on the non-equivalent control group design.

There are two basic kinds of information to be reported in order to do justice to any version of Design 3. First, there must be data showing how successfully the design was implemented. Second, the results of the outcome measures must be reported for both E-group and C-group and the appropriate comparisons made.

Reporting about implementation of the design

Showing how successfully the design was implemented will involve considering the following questions:

1. *Location of a reasonable comparison group.* If Design 3 results are to be interpretable, *just any* comparison group won't do. You should answer these questions: How do the E- and C-groups differ in background— SES, academic ability, attitude toward work or schooling, family stability, ethnicity? How did they happen to become part of the E- or C-group? Be particularly wary of volunteerism and selection based on extreme scores; these open you to challenge based on the enthusiasm and self-awareness of volunteers and the differential effects of regression in groups with different backgrounds.

2. *Program implementation.* Did the E-group receive the program? This question will be answered in the section of your report where you describe what the program looked like in operation.

3. *Contamination.* Did the C-group *not* get the program or any piece of it? That is, was contamination avoided? This requires at least some documentation of what happened in C-group classrooms.

4. *Confounds.* Were confounds avoided? Can you assess that there were no consistent differences between what happened to the E-group and

C-group other than Program X, differences which might reasonably be expected to either raise or lower scores on the outcome measures?

5. *Attrition.* Was there any difference between the *number* of cases lost from the E-group and number of cases lost from the C-group? Was there any difference in the *kinds* of cases (students, classrooms, teams, or schools etc.) which had to be dropped from the analysis in each group? A table[5] such as that shown below provides an appropriate summary and can be included in your report.

TABLE 5
Number of Students Dropped
from the Analysis for Various Reasons

Reason	Number dropped from E-group	Number dropped from C-group
Absent for posttest		
Absent from school during the program		
Removed from group at request of parent		
Left the school		
Other reasons		
Total number dropped		

Note that if the loss of cases is similar in both the experimental group and the non-equivalent control group, then this is further evidence for the similarity, and therefore comparability, of the two groups.

Analyzing, reporting, and discussing outcomes from Design 3

Tables and graphs. Below is a table for reporting results from Design 3, the non-equivalent control group, pretest-posttest design.

N is the number kept for analysis, which is equal to the number of cases for which there were pretest results minus the total number dropped from the analysis. The column labeled "Mean" contains the mean scores for each group on each test. The standard deviation (SD) related to each mean is reported in the adjacent column. You can describe outcomes between

TABLE 6
Pre- and Posttest Results
for the Experimental and Control Groups

	N	Pretest			Posttest		
		Mean	SD	t-test of difference	Mean	SD	t-test of difference
E-group							
C-group							

the groups either by performing a t-test on the obtained difference or by calculating its confidence limits. The t-test of difference in Table 6 is a test of the significance of the difference between the mean scores for the experimental and control groups on the pretest and posttest. The appropriate t-test to be used is the t-test for unmatched groups, sometimes called the non-correlated t-test.

Example

TABLE M
Pretest and Posttest Results
for the Experimental and Control Groups

	N	Pretest			Posttest		
		Mean	SD	t-test	Mean	SD	t-test
E-group	32	60	10	.90	90	9	5.1*
C-group	35	58	8		80	7	

*statistically significant at .05 level

The example illustrates the way Design 3 results are interpreted. The t-test for pretest scores was not significant, and this is indicated by *lack of* an asterisk. This means that on the pretest the two groups were more or less equivalent; any difference between the means was no more than one would expect due to chance. It is critical that you demonstrate this lack of significant initial difference when using Design 3. Having established that the groups were equivalent to begin with, you can then look at results after the program and compare the two group means, again by using a t-test. For the example shown, there is a large difference between the posttest means. Not surprisingly the t-test shows it to be significant, that is, bigger than could have been expected to occur by chance. For the example shown, the evaluator will write in his report:

> Mean pretest scores of the two groups were found to be *not*
> significantly different. This finding, and other information about
> the control group which we have been able to present, permit
> the conclusion that the control group participants were, at
> the outset, much like the E-group participants. This is at
> least true regarding most characteristics related to this study.
> After the program, however, the mean posttest score of the
> experimental group was significantly higher than the C-group's
> mean score. This gain can be attributed to their participation
> in the program. There remains, of course, the possibility that
> there were initial differences between the two groups which
> we have been unable to identify, and that these differences
> accounted for some of the posttest differences.

In addition to, or instead of, the table results from Design 3 can be displayed graphically. Graphs are more quickly understood than tables and should be used whenever possible, particularly if you must present data to a live audience. Probably the best graph to present for Design 3 is one like the following. It should be used, however, only if the pretest was the same test or an equivalent or parallel form of the posttest.

If the pretest was a test other than the one used as the posttest—an achievement or aptitude test, for instance—and if you found no significant difference on the pretest, then display posttest scores only. This simple display is also probably the clearest.

Comparing pretest scores. If there is *no significant difference* between the E-group and C-group *pretest* scores, that is very fortunate. This result is critical to the credibility of Design 3 as presented here. Of course, the groups might be different in other critical ways not measured by the pretest, but at least you can demonstrate that the groups were similar at first on a factor having an important effect on the posttest. Your case for

Example

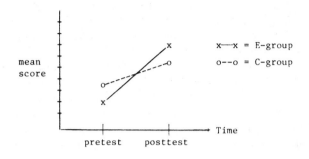

Figure J. Mean scores of the E-group and C-group on the pretest and posttest

Example

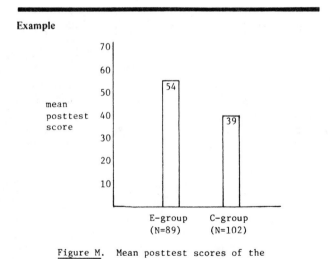

Figure M. Mean posttest scores of the E-group and C-group

initial equivalence of groups will most favorably affect the credibility of your overall study, of course, if you have chosen a pretest measure that is strongly correlated with the posttest.

If there *is* a significant difference in the *pretest* scores, then you have a problem. The quickest way around it is to note the problem, but proceed anyway. Graph the results and examine the *trends*. Note in your report that any apparent trends could be due to initial differences between the groups and the evaluation should be repeated, if possible, with a true control group. Note that despite the non-equivalence of the control group, it does provide at least some comparable data.

There are three other ways to work around the problem of significant pretest differences. Each procedure has problems of interpretation associated with it and at least a small group of research theorists who consider the procedure worthless. But as a practical matter it is good to try one or more of these rather than abandon attempts to use your results. It is even more informative to use all of them:

1. *Analysis of covariance* (ANCOVA). This technique will adjust the eventual *posttest* scores you obtain up or down according to pretest performance. It essentially subtracts statistically the effects of widely differing pretest scores from the posttest. It requires a considerable amount of computation and some rather rigorous assumptions should be met. It is only useful, for instance, if you can construct a strong case that the members of the experimental and control groups, though not assigned randomly, are so alike that the groups are as-good-as random anyway. ANCOVA is probably worth doing only if you have easy access to a data analyst and a computer.

2. *Post-hoc matching.* This procedure boils down to *re-selection* of a control group composed of people as like the E-group as possible. To match post hoc: Obtain a full set of pretest scores for each group, the E-group and the non-equivalent C-group. For each case (person, classroom) in the E-group, try to find a case in the C-group with the same or very nearly the same pretest score. Make a list of these matched pairs, recording their *post*test scores on the list. When you have the longest list possible, having matched pretest scores to within a few points of each other, apply a t-test for matched groups to the posttest scores or calculate confidence limits.

3. *Analysis of gain scores.* This method takes pretest differences into account in a rough but simple way. The *gain* is the posttest score minus the pretest score, assuming that both pre- and posttests were either the same tests, or parallel forms. Record gain scores for each student (or "case"). Then treat the gain scores as an ordinary set of scores and apply the t-test for unmatched groups.

Comparing posttest scores. If the posttest scores are significantly different and if the pretest scores were *not* significantly different, then you have good evidence that the different programs are producing different results.

In this case, report the significance of the size of the obtained difference, but please be careful to consider whether the difference is of any practical significance. Statistical significance, after all, only tells you that your results are not likely to have occurred by chance. It does not tell you if your results are of great magnitude, or if they are important enough to influence anybody. You should accompany any report of results, whether for formative or summative evaluation purposes, with an assessment of the likely *value* of the differences you have uncovered. Pages 75 to 77 describe the issue in greater detail.

If the pretest scores were more or less equivalent and the *posttest scores* were *not* significantly different, then you should conclude that there were no differential effects from the different programs. However, if the trends in results look promising even though non-significant, you might want to have a data analyst try a more powerful analysis. This person could perform an analysis of covariance (ANCOVA) or analysis of variance (ANOVA) using the pretest as a blocking factor. Analysis of covariance is a statistical technique used to adjust posttest scores to what they would have been had pretest scores been equivalent. It relies on a considerable number of assumptions about the nature of the test and the people taking it, and is therefore *not* a totally credible procedure.

If *objectives-based tests* or *attitude instruments* were used, you might have to report results in narrative or graphic form. For instructions about how to do this, refer to pages 78 to 80.

Summary of analysis, reporting, and discussion for Design 3

In reporting the results of a non-equivalent control group design, discuss first the extent to which the design was adequately implemented: Were confounds and contamination kept in check? What was the extent of attrition?

Because groups were not assigned randomly, you will need to present all the evidence you can find or produce to show that the groups were initially alike in characteristics that might have affected your results. The more convincingly you can argue that the members are so alike that the groups are as-good-as randomly composed, the more solid will be your eventual results. A major source of convincing evidence will be a non-significant difference among pretest scores, but you should present other characterizations of the groups as well, such as socioeconomic status and ability levels.

If the design has been adequately implemented, you will then present results and discuss whether or not the posttest difference between E- and C-groups was statistically significant. If performance differences between the E- and C-groups were statistically significant, you should consider their practical or educational significance.

NOTES

1. The important question of "unit of analysis" is described briefly on pages 140 to 144.

2. Another attrition table, applied to a somewhat different situation, appears on page 83.

3. Which of these units is randomly assigned depends on the level—individual, class, school, or even district—at which program impact will be judged. "Units of analysis" are discussed further on page 140.

4. An alternative attrition table showing loss of students for various reasons, as well as more extensive discussion of the attrition problem, appears on page 68.

5. Alternative attrition tables, as well as more extensive discussion of the problem of loss of cases, appear on pages 68 and 83.

For Further Reading

Cooke, T. D., & Campbell, D. T. (1976). The design and conduct of quasi-experiments and true experiments in field settings. In M. D. Dunnette (Ed.), *Handbook of industrial and organizational psychology.* Chicago: Rand McNally College Publishing. This article contains an extensive and clearly presented description of quasi-experimental designs on the order of Design 3.

Chapter 5

Designs 4 and 5:
The Time Series Designs

In this chapter, Design 4 is described in detail. Design 5 is described briefly since most of the procedures and interpretations for Designs 3 and 4 apply to Design 5 as well. A diagram, flowchart of essential steps, and some examples introduce each design.

Design 4:
The Single Group
Time Series Design

Diagram

	Time					
	1	2	3	4	5	6
Experimental Group	O	O	O	X	O	O	O

Summary

An instrument related to the program that will eventually be implemented is administered at regular intervals before the program begins, during the program, and then after it ends.

The Essential Steps in Implementing Design 4

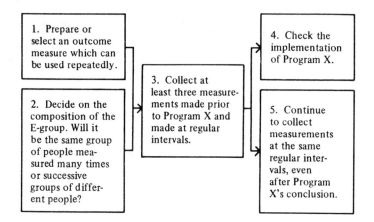

1. Prepare or select an outcome measure which can be used repeatedly.

2. Decide on the composition of the E-group. Will it be the same group of people measured many times or successive groups of different people?

3. Collect at least three measurements made prior to Program X and made at regular intervals.

4. Check the implementation of Program X.

5. Continue to collect measurements at the same regular intervals, even after Program X's conclusion.

Examples of Design 4 in Use

Three examples are presented for this design. In each example, the group which is measured is the group which gets the program, but with these differences:

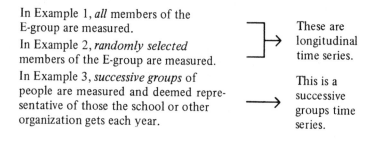

In Example 1, *all* members of the E-group are measured.

In Example 2, *randomly selected* members of the E-group are measured.

These are longitudinal time series.

In Example 3, *successive groups* of people are measured and deemed representative of those the school or other organization gets each year.

This is a successive groups time series.

Example 1. Longitudinal time series: Whole E-group measured each time. One objective of a fifth grade math program required students to be able to write down any multiplication table in a specified, short period of time. Each teacher gave biweekly speed tests to his entire class, but very few students were achieving the objective. The math supervisor suggested an intervention (Program X). She brought a group of junior high students to one fifth grade classroom each day for two weeks. Each junior high student spent fifteen minutes drilling one student, then fifteen minutes drilling another student on the multiplication tables. The teacher continued to give the speed tests after this intervention. The supervisor plotted the following graph from the teacher's records:

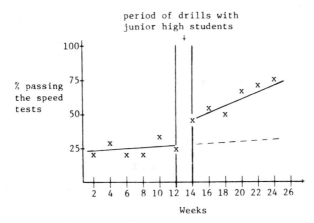

The trend line indicated that without the program, a far smaller percentage of the class would have passed the speed tests. It seemed that the program not only gave the percentage passing a boost, but also increased the *rate* of improvement. Perhaps the program had shown students how to work on this task. The supervisor was encouraged to try this intervention in other classrooms.

Example 2. Longitudinal time series: Random sample of E-group measured. A company's personnel director was concerned with building up the employees' pride and interest in the company and fellow workers. He planned to have a "This Is Your Company" week involving talent shows, lunch hour sports, department open houses, and so on. Rather than rely on subjective observations to indicate how successful this activity was, he decided early in the year to monitor employees' feelings about their work on a regular basis. He composed a questionnaire which was designed to measure the employee's current ("this week") attitude toward work. Every third week, he randomly selected eight employees from each department and administered the questionnaire to them in the cafeteria. Each time he summed up all the positive responses and recorded the score on a graph. His graph looked like this:

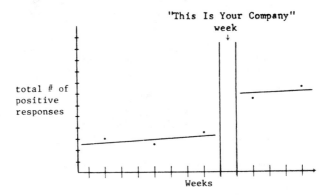

He was very pleased to note an apparent change in level. Following Program X, the number of positive responses was generally higher. The change in average level from before to after was greater than the general fluctuations found in the number of positive responses. He made a presentation to the Chief Executive Officer, who evidenced considerable interest in his "This Is Your Company" activities.

Example 3. Successive groups time series. A new "modular" math program was implemented two years ago at Grant High School. Rather than being assigned to a math class for an entire semester or year, students took a series of six-week math skills modules assigned on the basis of which skills they needed to master. They could repeat a module as many times as necessary to master the skill. The program was expensive because of administrative costs (extra tests, more frequent change of classes, etc.), extra teachers, and some new materials.

Board members, looking for a place to cut costs, raised questions about the effectiveness of the program, suggesting that it might be dropped. The district evaluator was asked to prepare a full report. Among the data he presented were scores on a standardized math test. Fortunately, the same test had been given for the last seven years, providing comparable data. He presented the following graph to the Board:

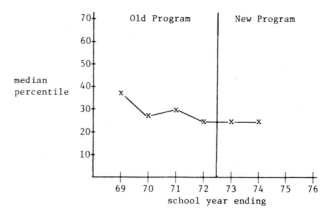

Figure H. Median percentile rank on the standardized math test at the end of the school year

The Board was not particularly pleased, but agreed to continue the program a little longer since, it was argued, the program needed more time to become fully effective. At least no severe drops had occurred after implementation of the program.

Presentation and Analysis of Data for Design 4

Two kinds of information will need to be reported in order to describe accurately your use of Design 4: data showing successful *implementation* of the design and *outcome* data.

Reporting about implementation of the design

Before you examine the *results* of the repeated time series measurements, it is essential to consider how accurately the design's prescription about whom and when to measure has been carried out. Here are some questions you will need to ask yourself before analyzing the numerical data:

1. *Did the program actually take place, and if so, when?* This question will be answered in the section of your report in which you describe what the program looked like in operation. For a time series design, the exact dates or times of the beginning and ending of the program must also be confirmed.

2. *Were there any confounds?* Did any events take place at or near the time the program started which could reasonably have influenced the measurements made?

Example. An algebra teacher has been monitoring with monthly tests the progress of one class of students. A new textbook was introduced in January, and monthly test scores have jumped considerably. The teacher would be inclined to think the new math text is the cause. Suppose, however, this particular class underwent a schedule change: Also in January, math instruction was moved from 11 a.m. to 8:30 a.m. It could be argued that morning alertness has caused the higher monthly scores, rather than the new materials. There is probably no way to decide which is the correct explanation; the new schedule is a *confound* making the results of the program impossible to assess.

A *large number of cases* gives some protection against confounds. Had the algebra teacher been monitoring many classrooms, it would be unlikely that they all received new schedules coincident with the new materials.

Discovering confounds and evaluating whether or not they seriously threaten the interpretation of results is a difficult and situation-specific task. Common sense is your best guide when considering the effects of confounds for your report. One method of examining a confound is to pay careful attention to the *speed* of changes you observe. If it seems reasonable to expect that a program will produce a *rapid* change, then its effects can probably be distinguished from confounds that produce a *slow* change.

Example. A factory introduced a longer lunch period. Soon afterwards, complaints increased about employee tardiness after lunch. Some people said it was due to the increased time available to go off site for lunch and then be late; others thought it was the result of increased number of new, younger workers. Examining time series records of tardiness after lunch time could show whether the number of offenses suddenly increased with the sudden introduction of the longer lunch or slowly increased with the slow change in the work-force composition.

3. *Was there a change in the method of obtaining the measurements or observations at or about the time of the intervention?* If, for example, the personnel director who introduced a longer lunch hour had simultaneously instructed his foreman to refer to him any employees who were tardy after lunch, then one would expect an increase in referrals simply because of his instructions, regardless of the effect of the longer lunch hours.

   Remember: For accurate conclusions to be drawn from a time series design, the method of measurement must remain the same throughout the series of measurements.

4. *Has the composition of the E-group changed during the experiment?* If you are using a *longitudinal* time-series design, you need to consider the problem of *loss or change of cases.* If the introduction of the program causes some cases (people, teams, etc.) to drop out of the group being measured, then this alone could influence the measurements.

Example. The teacher of an afterschool high school composition class for students who needed remedial help initiated a program based on copying the writing styles of popular magazines. He periodically assessed attitudes about the program and found that they grew more and more positive. Before he could present this apparently good result for judgment, however, he needed to ask if the *kinds of students composing the group* also changed. Perhaps some students who needed remediation didn't like the program and dropped out. Perhaps the program then attracted people for whom it was *not* intended—those who wrote pretty well and enjoyed it already. If this were the case, then the teacher's measures were no longer based on the same group. To assess the impact of the program the composition teacher will have to look separately at the data for *those who remained throughout.* This means eliminating the earlier data from those who later dropped out of the program and the later data from those who were not enrolled at the beginning.

If you are using a *successive groups* time series design, you will need to consider carefully if the composition of the groups themselves is likely to change at or about the time when you are expecting to see changes due to the program. Rapid changes in the characteristics of students entering a grade level can result, for instance, from the opening of a new industry in the neighborhood, from establishment of a large professional enterprise such as a college nearby, from flight to the suburbs, and so on. Such demographic changes affect the kinds of students who compose successive groups. If the population in question is changing, either rapidly or slowly, it will be hard to distinguish between the effect of any program and the effects of these changes.

One way to diminish the problem of a changing population is to make other measurements on the groups *in addition to* measurements intended to show the effect of the program. For example, if you were keeping records of secretaries' typing rates before and after the introduction of a new word processing program, you could also collect other data—say, shorthand rates—across the same time period. If the typing rates showed a positive jump with the introduction of the new program but the shorthand rates *did not*, this would support your argument that it was the program that caused the change rather than the composition of the group.

5. *Was the program introduced in response to a crisis?* Crises usually pass and things return to normal. If you have introduced a new program in response to a crisis, it was probably only one of many responses made by people to the crisis. When things get better, it is hard to argue that the program and only the program caused it. The many other attempts made at alleviating a bad situation are confounds. Besides, the improved situation could be a result of the normal run of events; things generally can only get better after being very bad.

Examining, reporting, and discussing outcomes from a time series design

If you are convinced that the design has been adequately implemented, and there seems a good chance of drawing conclusions from the repeated measures you have administered, then examine the data. The word *examine* is used here rather than *analyze* because a statistical analysis of time series data is complex and would have to be purchased from a statistician. Tentative conclusions can be made from plotting a graph and examining the data, however, and a graph is strong enough evidence for most evaluations.

Time series graphs. Time series data can best be examined when presented graphically. The following steps describe the graphing procedure:

1. For each set of scores collected at one time or collected during one time period, compute a summary statistic such as the total, the mean, the median, or the percentage responding a particular way. If the outcome measure is based on data extracted from records, you may want to consider carefully how to group the data. A record of absences, for

example, could be based on daily totals; but weekly totals would probably show less fluctuation and produce a clearer graph.

2. Make a graph in which the vertical axis represents scores on the outcome measure and the horizontal axis represents time.

3. Mark the times of observations at proper intervals along the horizontal axis.

4. Using the vertical axis, plot the outcome measure summary statistics for the times to which they apply.

5. Mark on the graph the beginning of the program and the end if the program ended during the observation period.

Example. A table of time series data

TABLE R
Mean Scores of the E-Group
on the Outcome Measure

	Time					
	Before program			After program		
	Jan	Feb	Mar	Apr	May	June
E group mean score	20	25	30	50	55	60

Example. A graph drawn from the table

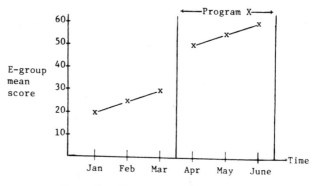

Figure K. Mean scores of the E-group

The effect of Program X can be assessed by seeing if the scores obtained after Program X was implemented, tended to be different from those obtained before. One way to detect a change in the trend of scores is to *draw a line* representing the before scores and another representing after. This procedure is described in the section called "Drawing the lines."

Once lines have been drawn, the graph can be examined for two major kinds of effects: a *trend* change or a *level* change (a jump). An alteration in slope or trend means that the *rate* of change of scores has been affected. A jump in the level or height of the graph might indicate a sudden increase or decrease in scores. Of course, both effects might occur. Examine the examples for illustrations.

Example of a trend change.

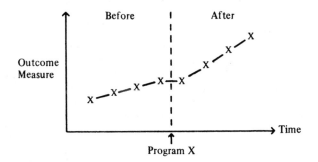

After Program X, scores increased more rapidly—there was a change in the upward *trend.*

Example of a jump. This graph shows a change in level, but no change in trend.

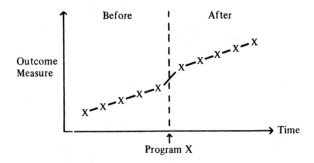

Program X appeared to cause a jump. After the jump, the trend continued at the same rate; that is, the before and after graphs are parallel.

Example of both a jump and trend change.

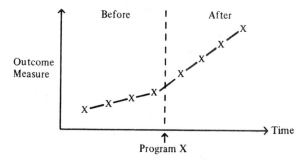

Note that in addition to the jump, the slope or trend of scores altered after the program.

Drawing the lines. In order to interpret time series results, you'll need to draw the best straight line through the scores obtained *before* Program X was implemented and the best straight line through the scores obtained *after* Program X was implemented.

The simplest method for drawing the best straight line to represent a trend in several scores uses a piece of thread as shown in the illustration. Adjust the thread until it seems to best represent the trend in the observations.

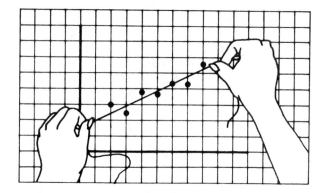

When you are adjusting the thread's position, imagine that each dot on the graph is attached to the thread by a rubber band. Put the thread into the position you think would best balance the thread between the scores. Do this for the pre-program scores, those during the program, and those obtained after the program, if there are any.

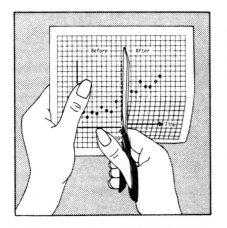

Since fitting a trend line by using a thread is not a totally objective procedure, it is wise to take the following precaution against possible bias *before* you undertake the thread procedure:

1. Make a copy of the graph.

2. Cut the copy in two along the "Program X" line.

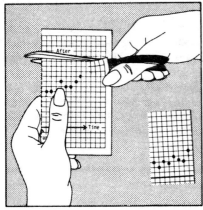

3. Trim the graph so that it is not clear which piece is the *before* and which the *after* part.

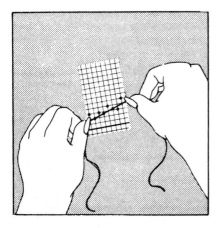

4. Then have someone who is not involved with the project fit the best straight line on each half.

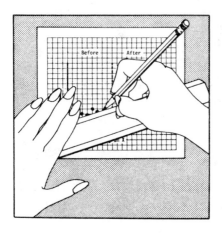

5. Copy the two trend lines back onto the original graph as accurately as possible.

6. You now have two independently estimated trend lines, one for *before* and one for *after* the implementation of Program X.

Please notice that in the diagrams above, points used for constructing the best straight line had already lined themselves up quite neatly. This rarely happens. The diagrams are drawn this way for clarity and they sacrifice realism.

A good way to aid your interpretation of a time-series graph is to *extrapolate* pre-program trends to show your best guess about what the results *might have been* without the program. The example below does this extrapolation by extending the *before* trend line into the *after* region.

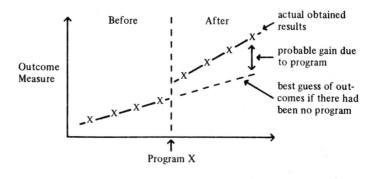

Example of extrapolation of a trend line

To extrapolate, lay a ruler along the before trend line and draw in a dotted line along the ruler in the after region:

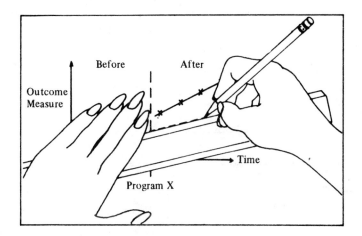

Interpreting time series graphs with extrapolation. In reporting time-series data, you can suggest that it was the program that brought about the gap between the *expected* outcomes, as located by the extrapolated trend line, and the outcomes you obtained. However, you need to consider several possible problems:

1. *Was there some other change at or about the same time as the program that could have caused the change from before to after?* It is wise to suggest other possible causes and discuss the likely extent of their contribution to the outcomes. The problem of dealing with confounds was discussed above and can be recalled by these questions:

   • Did the composition of the group stay the same?

   • Did the method of measurement stay the same?

   • Were there events other than the program which could have affected the group?

   • Was there a crisis at the time the program was introduced?

2. *Was the use of straight lines appropriate?* Perhaps if Program X had not occurred, a graph of the scores you obtained would have looked like this:

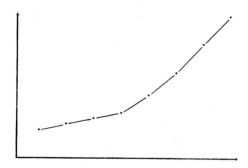

In this case, using a straight line for extrapolation has misled you.

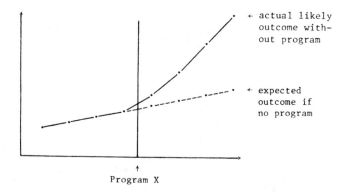

← actual likely outcome with- out program

← expected outcome if no program

Program X

The straight dotted line you drew grossly underestimates what scores would have been without the program. It makes a program that in reality had no effect look very good. Unfortunately, it is not possible to be sure whether the use of straight lines is appropriate or to be sure what the results would have been without the program. This is a weakness of the time-series, single group, design. Because this design has such logical loopholes and is not as powerful as the true experimental design, Design 1, it is called *quasi-experimental.*

3. *Could it be that the results reflect some cyclical pattern rather than a change due to the program?* Achievement, perhaps, always picks up in the second half of the school year, new program or no new program, and in business, employee, and customer behavior can also reflect seasonal changes. Be wary of this possibility if your time series is longitudinal. If you are using a successive groups design and you have

reason to suspect cyclical variation, then try to confine data collection to similar points on each cycle. For example, if there is a yearly cycle, compare test scores from May with test scores from other Mays, not with test scores from September.

Sometimes the "it would have happened anyway" argument can be examined by plotting an additional set of data. For example, perhaps you've been examining math scores for successive groups and they show a dramatic gain after a new program. Someone argues, "But the groups of students coming in were just of higher ability. It wasn't the program at all." To check on this suggestion, plot *reading* scores for the successive groups:

Example

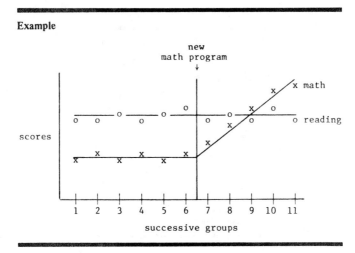

If reading didn't also show a jump, this strengthens the argument that it was the math program, not the pool of students, which caused the observed change. The same strategy will work for a *longitudinal* time series design, except that here you will be graphing reading and math for the *same* group over time. This can insure you against the cyclic variation argument during a single school year.

4. *Are the results too unstable to permit conclusions to be drawn?* If the scores or observations are all over the place and variable because of instability in the measurement instruments themselves, then it might not be possible to detect the results of even a successful program. In the absence of clear trends, some statistical help might be in order. The statistical analyses of time series data are beyond the scope of this book, however, and not yet in wide use. If your time series study is inconclusive, you might decide to set up a more powerful test of the program, one employing a control group design if possible.

Further analyses of the time series design. To enhance your analysis, you might try plotting the mean outcome scores not for the whole group, but for *parts* of the group. Doing this will give you an idea of whether the program affected people with different characteristics differently. Perhaps the program was particularly good—or damaging—for students of high or low ability, or for men but not women. Perhaps the program was good or poor for different people for unknown reasons.

To separate the patterns of scores for *high and low ability students,* you should first divide the group into high and low ability by some measure *other than the measure whose scores you are plotting* (this will avoid the influence of regression). Then plot separate time series graphs for the high and low ability groups.

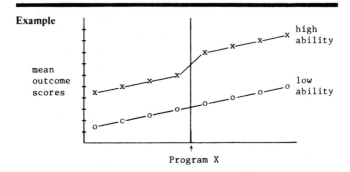

This graph indicates that Program X made a difference for the high ability student, but did not affect those of low ability.

To indicate the effects of the program on men and women separately, graph their scores separately:

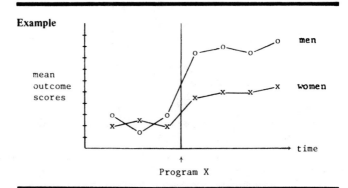

Please notice that the time series graph displays a summary statistic to represent the scores of a group. Usually this is the *average score* from each administration of an instrument. You should make sure that the summary statistic you use represents the group fairly. You may remember, for example, that averages are *not* good representatives of a group of scores when the range and variability of the individual scores are broad. If most people either scored very high on a test or failed it miserably, for instance, the resulting *mean* would actually *misrepresent* the situation. In cases where scores from single administrations of an instrument seem highly variable, you can modify the time series graph to depict this variability.

If you graph *medians,* show score variation by graphing the *upper* and *lower* quartile scores as well. The upper quartile is the raw score at the 75th percentile; the lower is the score at the 25th.

Example

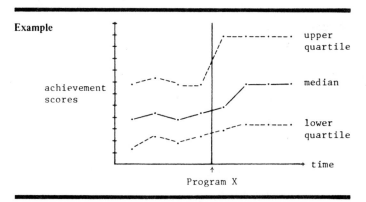

If you graph *mean* scores, then indicate the *standard deviation* for each mean. Do *not* plot highest and lowest scores. They are too unstable.

Example

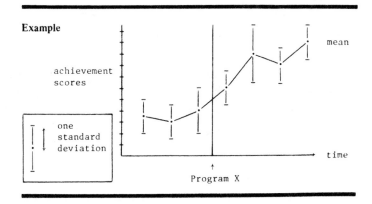

Design 5:
The Time Series with a
Non-Equivalent Control Group

Diagram

Time						
	1	2	3	4	5	6
Experimental Group	O	O	O	X	O	O	O
Non-Equivalent Control Group	O	O	O		O	O	O

Summary

Two groups which are similar but which were not formed by random assignment are measured at regular intervals before and after Program X is implemented. This design is just like Design 4—with the addition of a non-equivalent comparison group.

The Essential Steps in Implementing Design 5

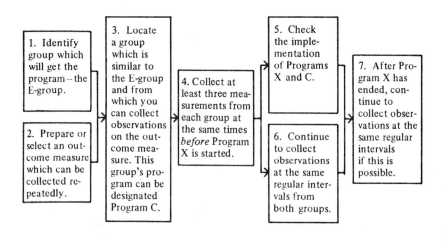

1. Identify group which will get the program—the E-group.

2. Prepare or select an outcome measure which can be collected repeatedly.

3. Locate a group which is similar to the E-group and from which you can collect observations on the outcome measure. This group's program can be designated Program C.

4. Collect at least three measurements from each group at the same times *before* Program X is started.

5. Check the implementation of Programs X and C.

6. Continue to collect observations at the same regular intervals from both groups.

7. After Program X has ended, continue to collect observations at the same regular intervals if this is possible.

Examples of Design 5 in Use

Example of a longitudinal time series with a control group. High school students were complaining that the study hall period was too short and requested that it be lengthened by fifteen minutes. Some staff members objected to this on the grounds that truancy resulted from allowing longer times out of class. Other staff disagreed and urged a longer afternoon study break on a trial basis. The principal realized that as warm, spring days were approaching, the amount of truancy would be going up no matter what the length of the study break. Consequently, she decided that simply to keep a record of the number of absences reported from afternoon classes would not be sufficient. She would need to compare trends at her school with trends at a similar school in order to allow for the general increase in absences which seemed imminent. After implementing the longer study hall for a trial four-week period, she searched her own records to find the number of absences which had occurred during afternoons throughout the previous weeks. She was able to persuade the principal of another school of equal size and comparable student body, but no afternoon study break, to search his records and provide her with the same set of statistics. She then plotted the following graph:

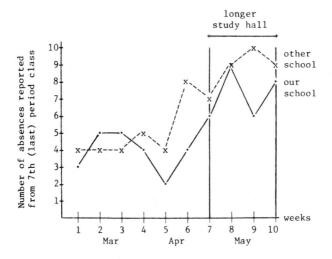

From these graphs the faculty and principal concluded that although there had been a rise in the number of absences, the longer study break was probably not the reason since the similar school nearby had experienced a rise at the same time. Notice how misleading the graph would have been without the addition of a non-equivalent control group.

Example of a successive groups' time series with a control group. A new method of training airline flight attendants to deal with emergency situations was planned and implemented at the West Coast Training Center of a major U.S. airline. In considering how to monitor the effectiveness of the program, the training center's director persuaded the East Coast Training Center to provide data on their students who continued to use the standard program. The West Coast director obtained data on four successive groups of trainees at each center prior to the implementation of the program in his center. The director also obtained data on both centers' trainees for four successive groups after the program's start-up on the west coast. The data were scores on two standard tests of how to deal with emergencies: a paper and pencil test and a simulation test. The West Coast Center director then graphed the combined scores of the eight successive classes of trainees at each center, as shown below over a period of two years. This provided a good index of the results the new program was producing.

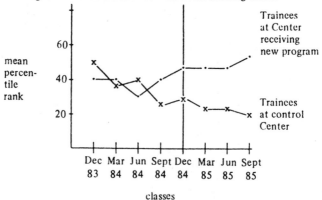

Figure C.   Mean percentile ranks of program and control groups on two combined tests of handling emergency situations administered over a two-year period

Analyzing, Reporting, and Discussing Outcomes from Design 5

Design 5 is just like Design 4 except that it adds an extra series of data, data from the non-equivalent control group. These data help you to rule out alternative explanations for changes in outcome measures which are found to coincide with the introduction of the experimental program.

Because Designs 4 and 5 are so similar, the reader is asked to read Design 4 for further guidance in executing and interpreting Design 5. Because you will be using a non-equivalent control group, read the section on Design 3 as well. Of course, if a *true control group* can be formed, the conclusions to be drawn from a time series design would be even stronger. In fact, a time series design with a true control group would be the strongest possible design.

Chapter 6

Design 6:
The Before-and-After Design

Design 6:
The Before-and-After Design

Design 6 is the least adequate design for conducting either formative or summative evaluation. It represents a choice to invest no effort in collecting comparison data which can be used to judge the quality of the program's results. Of course, in those *formative* evaluations where the focus is on monitoring adequate *implementation* of a program exclusively, absence of comparisons for judging outcomes is not a serious problem. The few summative evaluations which focus solely on adequacy of implementation also need not assess the quality of the outcomes produced. But in any evaluation situation where someone is likely to ask, "How good are the *results*?" "Is it the program which is causing them?" Design 6 will prove to be inadequate. In such an evaluation, particularly a summative one, then, every effort should be made to use one of the other designs. Design 6 should be considered only as a last resort.

Diagram

	Time	
	1 (pre)	2 (post)
Experimental Group	O X	O

Summary

The only people measured are those who get the program. They are pretested before the program and posttested afterwards.

The Essential Steps in Implementing Design 6

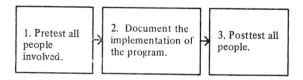

| 1. Pretest all people involved. | → | 2. Document the implementation of the program. | → | 3. Posttest all people. |

Example of Design 6 in Use

A Federal program example. ESEA Title I funds were available to four schools in a school district. All students were pretested with a standardized test at the beginning of the year and posttested with the same test at the end of the year. Using forms provided by the State Department of Education, the evaluator reported "gains" made over the year, subtracting average pretest scores from posttest scores per subject matter area.

Interpreting results from the Before-and-After Design, Design 6, presents severe problems because the design doesn't help you to know *what kind of results might have been obtained without the program.* It is therefore almost impossible to say for sure whether the obtained results are good or bad. Having neither a control or comparison group nor a time series of measures on the experimental group, the evaluator loses the chance to detect the small but important gains which are perhaps all that can be realistically expected from a year or so of a new program.

However, since Design 6 is by no means uncommon, this chapter aims to help you locate whatever narrow silver lining can be wrenched from behind this cloudy design. One speck of silver comes, of course, from the time saved by not having to monitor two groups. Because there is only one group to measure, the evaluator can make more measurements, ferret out more information, delve more deeply into the activities produced by the program. Because of this, the evaluator implementing Design 6 should do a good job of *describing* the program, outlining in detail its materials and activities. These can be related in turn to the theoretical base underlying the program—the rationale for the means by which the program was supposed to achieve its objectives. The evaluator can at least, then, assess whether the program *looks in operation as it is supposed to.* Since data are unavailable about the extent to which the program contributed to any measured outcomes, the question of whether such program implementation causes good results will, of course, have to be left unanswered.

Analyzing and Describing Outcomes from Design 6

Design 6 is often used with norm-referenced achievement tests. Scores on these tests can be converted to standard scores or other *normed* scores that compare the performance of a certain group of students with the test results for a national sample of students at the same grade level. This feature of normed tests gives you a means of interpreting the pretest and posttest results relative to the performance of that standardization group. Please remember, though, that the difference between the skills measured by the test and the skills taught in the program is frequently great enough to make scores on norm-referenced tests incapable of reflecting the program's true accomplishments.

Displaying the results from standardized tests

The evaluator can report scores on standardized tests in a table such as the one shown here:

Example

TABLE P

Mean Pretest and Posttest Reading and Math Scores
for Schools in the XYZ Program

Group	n^a	Pretest	Posttest	t-test
		Reading		
School A	401	59.4	64.3	3.8*
School B	720	50.2	70.5	12.2*
School C	364	40.8	60.2	4.5*
		Math		
School A	461	63.2	70.1	2.4*
School B	726	58.4	71.2	3.1*
School C	362	32.9	33.4	-0.8

[a]Number present for both the pre- and posttests, and therefore the students on whose scores the t-test was calculated.

*Statistically significant at .05 level.

The results in the above table represent a situation in which the *same test* has been given as both a pre- and posttest. The t-test tests the significance of the difference between mean pre- and posttest raw scores and is a t-test for *matched* groups.

If the tests were cognitive achievement tests, and the program lasted any length of time, a significant difference between a pre- and posttest would be nearly always expected anyway. Students do better on any particular test as they grow older and accumulate experience. However, you might find a situation such as that shown for Math, School C in the example above: no significant difference between pre- and posttest math scores. In this case, someone should look into what has been going on in this school. Was there a testing error perhaps? Or are the students really making no progress?

Often in the Before-and-After Design situation, the evaluator has to report results for State or Federal agencies on forms which they supply. These forms frequently require the results of standardized, norm-referenced tests. In the event that the evaluator may also need to present the results of standardized, published, norm-referenced tests to *lay audiences,* the following section provides some pointers.

Suggestions for presenting standardized test scores to lay audiences

Before any scores are presented, make a few remarks about the nature of standardized achievement tests. Explain to your audience that it must make a conscious decision about how much importance it will attach to standardized test scores. The decision should be based on an awareness of how the tests were developed, an assessment of their overlap in content with the program being evaluated, and on a description of the norm group with whom the scores are being compared. Be sure that your presentation explains what a "norm" group is and emphasizes the following:

1. *Because of the nature of standardized tests, half the norm group students have to be "below average."* This is usually readily understood when percentile scores are mentioned, but it is forgotten when "grade equivalent" scores are discussed. Grade equivalent scores sound like criterion-referenced scores, *but they are not.* Standardized tests will never show everyone reading at or above grade level! Besides this easy misinterpretation, grade equivalent scores have certain statistical problems associated with them which render them of dubious accuracy. They should be *avoided* whenever possible.

2. *Standardized tests may not measure exactly what the program taught.* Unless someone has made a conscious effort to assure that the program covers the same material as the test,[1] or, conversely, has found a test that matches program content, a standardized test is not likely to assess the same skills your program teaches. Teachers, who do not usually have access to the tests, cannot often figure out the concepts and skills that the test taps; and therefore they cannot be sure to teach what the test measures. This means that the tests may be unfamiliar to students

and may miss many of the things students have learned. Standardized tests, then, may not be good indicators of either how much students know or of how well they have been taught.

Having warned against judging a program solely on the basis of standardized tests, you can present the test's results as one general indicator of student achievement in subject areas related to the program.

Suggestions for lending credibility to the Before-and-After Design

The activities described so far for implementing Design 6—description of program implementation, presentation of pre- and posttest data, testing for statistical significance, and presentation of standardized test results— represent the bare minimum necessary for lending the design credibility. Below are some further suggestions for examining and describing the program.

Be cautious in the choice of testing times if using standardized tests. As has been mentioned, one solution to the problem of the absence of a comparison group is to use standardized, norm-referenced achievement tests and compare the E-group results with scores of the nationally representative "norm" group. This comparison can be justified if you locate a standardized test that tests the material the program aims to teach. Even then, however, a standardized test should only be employed if you can build a case that the norm group students were similar to yours, and if you pretest and posttest the E-group *at the same times* during the school year—mid May, for instance, or early January—as the norm groups were tested. Information about the characteristics of the norm groups and the times they were tested should be provided in manuals available from publishers. It is necessary to be cautious about *times of testing* because norms which the publisher reports for testing occasions in between the dates when he *actually* tested the norm group are essentially guesses based on interpolation. They may be substantially inaccurate.

Look at different component emphases. Perhaps all the sites at which the program has been implemented are using the program resources in the same way so that you really are confronted with one homogeneous program. Perhaps, however, the program is somewhat different from site to site. Perhaps at one school, for example, parent involvement is heavily emphasized, whereas at another site a lot of funds have been used for staff development. Particularly if your role is formative, you might want to see if these *different emphases* are producing different, detectable results. You could treat sites with different emphases as non-equivalent control groups not for the whole program but for alternate sub-components or versions of the program. A chance for comparison could arise even if one site allocated more time to reading than did another site—you might want to see if the extra time spent on reading appeared to improve reading posttest scores. In these cases, read the directions for Design 3.

Examine the differential impact of the program on people with different characteristics. Examine how the program has affected people of different ability levels, or different sexes, or with different attendance rates, or whom teachers rate as highly motivated as opposed to poorly motivated. By splitting up and examining the results from various subgroups, you might find indications of the people for whom the program is working best or worst. This applies to attitude measures as well as to ability measures. This "splitting up" will demand one of two statistical treatments: you can compare the mean results for various groups using statistical tests, or you can calculate a correlation coefficient to detect a relationship between individual characteristics (e.g., number of days in attendance) and outcomes (e.g., achievement, or positive attitude).

Develop and try out many instruments which might be sensitive measures of the goals of the program. If your relationship with the program— or programs of its type—will be a long one, then use some of your time to find or produce tests more sensitive to its intended effects. Have well-designed, field-tested instruments ready at the end of your evaluation, and push hard to have at least a non-equivalent control group the next time you work as an evaluator in the particular setting.

If at all possible, focus the evaluation on attainment of objectives. If program *goals* can be broken down and spelled out as *objectives,* then you can write or find tests to measure attainment of these objectives. In some cases, you might even be able to use a standardized test to measure attainment of program objectives.

By focusing on objectives, you can render more specific the information your evaluation provides:

- You will be able to point out the program's strong and weak areas by reporting which objectives many people mastered and which objectives many people failed to master.

- You can ask experts or staff to rate the objectives in terms of their importance, so that you can concentrate on accurate measurement of the most important ones.

- You can ask experts or staff to set passing criteria which seem to represent reasonable requirements for demonstrating mastery. The number of people meeting objectives according to these criteria can then be used as a yardstick to judge program success or failure. There are a couple of serious objections to this procedure, but it is still much better than simply looking at a single aggregate score and trying to interpret it. One objection to evaluating a program in terms of criteria set by the staff is that it is hard to tell whether success indicates program effectiveness or the setting of low standards. Likewise, lack of success could indicate a poor program, or it could mean that an ambitious, hopeful staff had set high expectations rather than low, easily reached ones.

If you choose to evaluate by objectives, you can construct or purchase *objectives-based tests*. These will allow you to report individual achievement per objective, displaying for your audience what was accomplished over the program's duration.

Regardless of whether you focus the evaluation on standardized test scores or achievement of objectives, however, you still must face the constant Design 6 problem: the absence of good reason to attribute successful attainment of the objectives to the program alone. Perhaps achievement gains were due to the natural growth of the individuals, or perhaps the failure to achieve objectives was due to a high absentee rate, not to a poor program.

Displaying results from objectives-based tests for Design 6

Bar graphs are a particularly useful way to present data about the achievement of objectives. With each bar representing one objective, a glance at the graph will show levels of student achievement.

Example. Figure A shows mean percentages of students achieving each of twelve objectives. The data are displayed in Table A. Notice how much easier it is to see the pattern of achievement from the graph.

TABLE A
Mean Percentage of Students in Program X Classrooms
Achieving the Twelve Objectives at Pretest

Group	Objective #											
	1	2	3	4	5	6	7	8	9	10	11	12
Ninth grades (N=23)	91	76	34	33	38	16	13	7	56	16	22	0

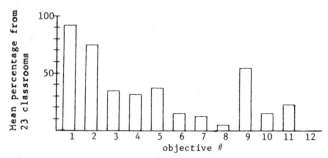

Figure A.   Mean percentage of students in Program X classrooms achieving the twelve objectives at pretest

Both pretest *and* posttest results can be shown using the same figure:

Example. In Figure B, the posttest results have been added as shaded bar graphs for each objective. The figure clearly shows for which objectives the number of students passing has increased. Gains have been made mainly in objectives 5, 6, and 7.

TABLE B
Mean Percentage of Students in Program X Classrooms
Achieving the Twelve Objectives at Pretest and Posttest

Group	Objective #											
	1	2	3	4	5	6	7	8	9	10	11	12
Ninth grades (N=23)												
pretest	91	76	34	33	38	16	13	7	56	16	22	0
posttest	77	62	43	41	66	35	30	11	30	7	7	2

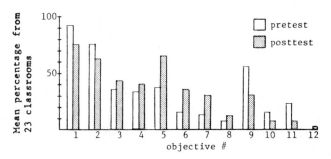

Figure B.   Mean percentage of students in Program X classrooms achieving the twelve objectives at pretest and posttest

At times, the amount of data may be so large that bar graphs are impractical. Perhaps converting a table of numbers into *symbols* will make presentation clearer even though you lose some detail.

Example. Table C presents objectives-based data in terms of percentage of employees passing per classroom, and Table D presents the same data interpreted differently. Note how the title changes. The first words of the title of a table usually refer to the numbers or symbols which are found in the body.

TABLE C
Percentage of Employees Passing the Objectives
in Each of the Text Processing Classrooms

Classroom	Creates file	Sets margins	Moves text	Prints file
1	99	85	83	70
2	98	87	82	60
3	98	80	78	65
4	90	78	60	69
5	95	82	72	79
6	99	90	87	80
7	92	85	60	65
8	98	82	90	76
9	99	87	84	70
10	99	87	81	62

The situation in which *goals* have been set regarding the percentage of persons who should pass various objectives produces additional graphing possibilities. For some objectives, the goal of a 100% pass rate may be set. When pilots are trained, for instance, the hope is that 100% of them will master safe landing practices. In education, it might be decided that all children should be able to read pill-taking instructions accurately or know how to make change. For other objectives, and for a particular grade level, the goal of a pass rate of 80% might be set. For some objectives, mastery might be expected from only 20% of the students. This might be the case with the enrichment part of a curriculum. Pass rate expectations provide a way of *grouping* objectives, as illustrated in the next example. The example also shows a neat way of displaying pre- and posttest pass rates by graphing posttest results as a shadow bar *behind* the pretest bar for each objective.

If a goal has been set that 80% of employees should achieve each objective, then the contents can be displayed as symbols:

TABLE D
Objectives Passed by 80% or More of the
Employees in the Ten Text Processing Classrooms

Classroom	Creates file	Sets margins	Moves text	Prints file
1	+	+	+	o
2	+	+	+	o
3	+	+	o	o
4	+	o	o	o
5	+	+	o	o
6	+	+	+	+
7	+	+	o	o
8	+	+	+	o
9	+	+	+	o
10	+	+	+	o

KEY: + = objective passed by 80% or more of the employees
o = objective passed by less than 80% of the employees

Example

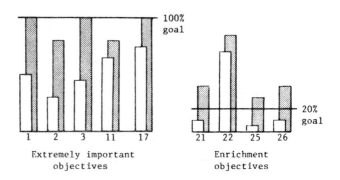

100% goal

20% goal

1 2 3 11 17
Extremely important
objectives

21 22 25 26
Enrichment
objectives

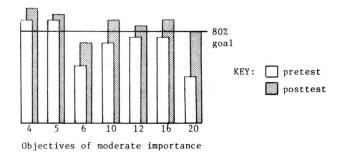

Figure F. The achievement of program objectives showing different goals for the percentage of students achieving the objectives

One can readily see from Figure F that

- the goal of 100% passing was not reached for objectives 2 and 11
- the goal of 80% passing was not achieved for objective 6
- all the 20% goals for enrichment objectives were achieved
- three goals had been achieved at pretest time–those for objectives 4, 5, and 22

NOTE

1. Though to some people the idea of using a standardized test to determine program content sounds like the presumably abhorrent practice of "teaching to the test," in many cases it is a good idea. If a standardized test will be the only measure of program outcomes, and if actual decisions about the program will be based on its results, then *someone* thinks its content is important. If the timing of your relationship with the program permits you to influence its content, then you would do the program a service to examine the test and alert its staff to the objectives (not the items themselves!) that the test seems to assess.

Chapter 7

A More Complex Design: Analysis of Variance (ANOVA)

The preceding chapters have dealt with designs involving only *two* treatment groups—the E-group and the C-group. This chapter introduces designs that can be applied to *three or more programs* and that can examine the influence of factors other than the program in producing the outcomes you obtain. Besides describing how an analysis of variance (ANOVA, pronounced AN-Ó-VA) can be set up, the chapter prepares you to talk to consultants who help you analyze ANOVA data. It will be important to consult with a person familiar with research and statistics as soon as you decide to attempt a complex design.

How to Set Up an ANOVA Matrix

Suppose your school district has *two* new programs, Program A and Program B—both in elementary reading—which need to be evaluated as alternatives to the regular program (Program C). Suppose further that the project personnel suspect that the results might vary for classrooms with different characteristics. The principal one that they feel will influence the effect of the program is *degree of structure*. The program may produce different results in open-structured classrooms as opposed to traditional classrooms. As district evaluator you need to answer the following evaluation questions:

1. The usual one—Do Programs A, B, and C have significantly different effects? Is one better than the others?

2. But also—Does the effectiveness of the three programs depend at all on the *kind of classrooms* in which they are implemented? For instance, is one program consistently better in open-structured classrooms whereas another is better in more traditional classrooms?

You have to assess the effects of two *factors,* each of which may be influencing results in reading: one factor is the *kind of program,* the other factor is a *characteristic of the classroom*—its structure. The way to set up a design to find out the effects of various factors is to set out the factors on two sides of a box:

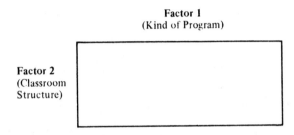

Next, write down the *levels* of each factor. The levels are the categories for that factor. In the example being discussed, there are *three* levels corresponding to the kind of program; these are A, B, and C. There are *two* levels for classroom structure, namely open-structured and traditional. These levels are written along the appropriate sides of the box, dividing it into *cells* and producing a typical ANOVA matrix, Table 7. Note that because there are three levels of one factor and two of another, the resulting box, or matrix, has 3 x 2 = 6 cells.

TABLE 7
ANOVA Matrix for a 3-by-2 Design

		Factor 1 (Kind of Program)		
		Level 1 (Program A)	Level 2 (Program B)	Level 3 (Program C)
Factor 2 (Classroom structure)	Level 1 (open-structured)	*cell #1*	*cell #2*	*cell #3*
	Level 2 (traditional structured)	*cell #4*	*cell #5*	*cell #6*

Table 7 is the basis for the design which is needed to answer the questions that have been posed: Do the programs have different effects? Do the programs act differently in open-structured as opposed to traditional classrooms? The next step is to find classrooms to put in each of the cells. Ideally, you will want to randomly distribute the three programs *evenly* among the open and traditional classrooms, though in practical situations this may not be possible. Suppose that, among the district's first grades, there were 8 open-structured and 13 traditional classrooms. Then you might have to assign these 21 classrooms as in this example:

Example. Distribution of classrooms to cells in a 3-by-2 ANOVA matrix

TABLE E

Number of First Grade Classes Assigned Randomly
to Cells of ANOVA Matrix for Examining
Program-by-Structure Relationship

		Kind of Program			
		Program Alpha	Program Beta	Program Cee-and -Say	
Classroom Structure	open struc- tured	N = 3	N = 2	N = 3	8
	tradi- tional struc- tured	N = 4	N = 4	N = 5	13
		7	6	8	21

The district has 13 traditional and 8 open-structured first grades. Enough materials were available for 7 Program Alpha and 6 Program Beta classes. *Which* classrooms got *which* programs was randomly determined. The 3 classrooms in the first cell are 3 open-structured classrooms that get Program Alpha. All together, 7 classrooms will implement Program Alpha: 3 open-structured and 4 traditional classrooms. Check the matrix and make sure you know what the numbers represent. For example, what is "21" in the lower right corner? Answer: the total number of classrooms.

This example illustrates the more usual, but less statistically desirable situation of *unequal cell sizes*—some cells have 2 or 3 cases; some have 4 or 5. Unequal cell sizes open an ANOVA to possible violations of the assumptions underlying its interpretation. You should strive for equal cell sizes wherever possible. The problems brought on by unequal assignment to cells in your situation can be explained by your data analyst. In the majority of cases, be assured, the problem is far less severe than troubles over *small* cell sizes—your alternative should you have to throw cases away to make the cells equal.

Remember that in the example, classrooms were *randomly* assigned to cells. Often, however, you will not be able to randomize easily. Sometimes, your evaluation must simply work with what is there, or you must *invite* teachers to try out new programs. In such situations, you can still fill the cells in the design, but *interpretation* of your results will be more difficult. For example, if the old program, Program Cee-and-Say, should turn out the best results, would this be because it *is* best; or could it be explained by the fact that teachers who were already getting good results with the regular program did not want to try anything new, so did not try Program Alpha or Beta? This would mean there was a *selection bias* influencing the results. The classrooms trying out the three programs were *not* equivalent. Because of the *voluntary* method of assigning programs, people who wanted a change chose the new programs, Alpha and Beta. Those in the old Cee-and-Say group were classrooms which had contented, and probably already quite effective, teachers.

Though non-random filling of the cells gives you some problems, it still allows you to use statistics to check against chance results. When the statistical test for analysis of variance is applied, differences among mean scores in the cells will *still* show whether non-random factors have influenced your results. That is, you will still be able to tell whether the differences in results obtained are too large to have been caused by chance. The problem, as has been said, will be to show that the factor causing the differences was the *program* and not something extraneous such as teachers' level of experience or students' class schedules.

Now suppose you have been able to *randomly* fill the cells of the design with classrooms as planned:

Example. Classroom assignments to cells of ANOVA indicated by teachers' names

TABLE F

Classes Assigned to Programs and Structures,
Identified by Teacher's Name

Kind of Program

		Program Alpha	Program Beta	Program Cee-and-Say
Classroom Structure	open structured	Jones Humphrey London	Ramirez Martin	Smith Ford Davis
	traditional structured	Ross Brown Higgins Reese	Phillips Johnson Graham Kelly	Chan Robinson Fitzgerald Cohen Carson

21

There are 3 classrooms in 2 of the open-structured cells and 2 in the other. Among traditional classrooms, programs Alpha, Beta, and Cee-and-Say receive 4, 4, and 5 classes, respectively. This adds up to a total of 21 classrooms.

It is hoped that while this particular tryout of the elementary reading program is in operation during its year-long existence, all 21 classrooms will *remain in their cells*; that is, open-structured classrooms will remain open-structured and classrooms supposedly getting Program Alpha will in fact get Program Alpha, and so forth. You will know whether these things have gone smoothly because checks on proper and consistent implementation of the programs, and vigilance for evidence of confounds, contamination, and attrition, will be part of your job as either formative or summative evaluator.

Now suppose that at the end of the year, a posttest is given in all classrooms and the mean score computed for each classroom. Thus, in the first cell, Ms. Jones's open-structured classroom getting Program Alpha might have a classroom mean raw score of 70 on the Comprehensive Test of Basic Abilities (CTBA) given in May. All you need to do now is give the 21 classrooms' mean scores to the data analyst and ask the analyst to provide you with an *analysis of variance* (ANOVA) for the design. "It's a 3-by-2 design with unequal cell sizes," you would tell the analyst. "The two factors are program (3 levels) and classroom structure (2 levels)."

If there is no data analyst available in the school district, a call to the nearest university could locate a graduate student in education or psychology who would be glad to perform this analysis for you, probably for a fee of no more than $60 or $80.

How to Interpret Results from an Analysis of Variance

Looking at Table F in the above example, suppose that in the first cell the classroom mean scores were:

Jones	70
Humphrey	75
London	65

In that case, the mean score for the cell is 70: $\frac{70 + 75 + 65}{3}$ = 70. This mean of the scores in the cell is called the *cell mean*. Suppose the scores in each cell were averaged to get all the cell means and those cell means looked like this:

Example

TABLE G

Cell Means for the Classrooms in Table F

	Program Alpha	Program Beta	Program Cee-and-Say
open structured	70	60	50
traditional structured	72	62	52

Now just by examining those results consider how you would answer your two evaluation questions:

1. Do the three programs have different effects?
2. Does the effectiveness of the programs depend on the kind of classroom in which they are implemented?

Looking across the first row (open classrooms) at the numbers 70, 60, 50, it seems clear that Program Alpha is associated with better results than Program Beta, and Beta in turn looks better than Program Cee-and-Say. Glancing across the second row (traditional classrooms) you can see the same pattern of descending scores—72, 62, 52. Looking down the *columns,* you'll find another consistent pattern: traditional classroom scores are slightly higher than open-structured classroom scores, without exception. In the situation illustrated, each *factor* has a consistent effect: each instance of Factor 1 (programs) makes about 10 points difference, and each of the two instances of Factor 2 (classroom structure) makes about 2 points difference. *But are these differences significant?* This is what the analysis of variance tells you. The ANOVA table provided by the data analyst might look like this:

Example

TABLE H

Analysis of Variance Table for Table G Data

Source	df	MS	F
program	2	764.77	37.01*
structure	1	16.81	0.82
program x structure	2	0.09	0.01
error	15	20.62	
Total	20		

*$p < .05$

This is what the ANOVA table tells you: Under the heading "Source," the factors of the design are listed: *program* type and classroom *structure.* "Source" means "source of variation" and it tells you which factor is being tested. In the first line of the table the program factor is being tested for significance. Following the first row across, there is a 2 under "df." This means that the degrees of freedom (df) for the first factor was 2. The degrees of freedom is always one less than the number of levels for the factor. In this case, there were 3 "levels" of program, so the df was 2. You do not have to worry about the meaning of this, but it is useful to check such figures to be sure no gross mistakes were made by the data analyst. "MS" stands for "mean square," something a bit too complicated for this discussion. Look at the last entry on the row, under "F." This number is the one which provides the test of significance. In this case, it has been determined to be significant at the .05 level indicated by the symbols $p < .05$. *This tells you that the program factor made a significant difference in results.* These particular results would have occurred by chance fewer than five times out of a hundred.

Checking the second row, the *structure* factor, you can see that the F-value was *not* significant; it has not been given an asterisk. This tells you that the differences between open-structured and traditional classrooms could indeed have occurred by chance. The differences are *not large enough* to be considered significant. However, this is a side issue; the difference between open-structured and traditional classrooms was not one of your evaluation questions. If you'll remember, these evaluation questions were:

1. Do programs Alpha, Beta and Cee-and-Say have significantly different effects?

2. Does the effectiveness of the three programs depend at all on the kind of classrooms in which they are implemented?

The first line of the ANOVA table answered the first evaluation question: Yes, the programs do have significantly different effects.

Now for the second question: Do the effects of the programs depend upon the kind of classroom structure? Put another way: Do a particular kind of program and a particular type of classroom structure *interact* to produce better or worse results? This question is answered by looking at the third line of the ANOVA table where *program x structure* is the source of variation. The fact that the F value in the third row is *not significant* means that whatever effects the programs had, these effects did not vary with the kind of classroom structure. Actually, this is already clear from simply looking at the cell means in the Table G example. That table shows the same pattern of scores for both the open and traditional classrooms. Open-structured classroom means showed the same consistent decrease (70, 60, 50) across programs as did those for the traditional classroom (72, 62, 52).

The third row of this ANOVA table is called the *interaction term* (a "first order interaction" to be precise). This row should actually be examined *first* because if the interaction term is significant, you cannot make general statements about the similar one-factor relationships appearing above, such as "Program Alpha is better than Beta or the Cee-and-Say Program." If there were a significant interaction in this example, for instance, you might have had to make separate statements about the effects of the programs: one statement about their effects in open-structured classrooms and another about the effects in traditional classrooms.

The following data displays illustrate the difference between a situation in which there *is* an interaction and a situation in which there is not. The displays compare the results just discussed with a similar set of results which show a significant interaction between the two factors.

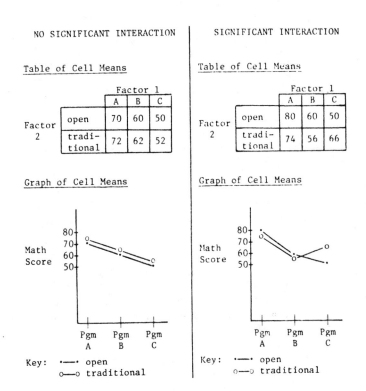

NO SIGNIFICANT INTERACTION

Table of Cell Means

Factor 2		Factor 1		
		A	B	C
	open	70	60	50
	tradi-tional	72	62	52

Graph of Cell Means

Math Score

80
70
60
50

Pgm A   Pgm B   Pgm C

Key: •—• open
       o—o traditional

SIGNIFICANT INTERACTION

Table of Cell Means

Factor 2		Factor 1		
		A	B	C
	open	80	60	50
	tradi-tional	74	56	66

Graph of Cell Means

Math Score

80
70
60
50

Pgm A   Pgm B   Pgm C

Key: •—• open
       o—o traditional

ANOVA Table

Source	df	MS	F
program	2	764.77	37.01*
structure	1	16.81	0.82
program x structure	2	0.09	0.01
error	15	20.62	
Total	20		

*p < .05

ANOVA Table

Source	df	MS	F
program	2	805.49	61.02*
structure	1	22.96	1.74
program x structure	2	213.80	16.20*
error	15	13.20	
Total	20		

*p < .05

Interpretation

1. There are significant differences among the three programs, A, B, and C. Significant results from a non-interaction factor are usually referred to as a significant main effect.

2. The effects of the program are not significantly influenced by the classroom structure. There is no interaction between the factors.

Interpretation

1. There appear to be significant differences somewhere among the three programs, A, B, and C. If you had equal cell sizes, you could report this significant main effect whether or not you obtained a significant interaction. If you have unequal cell sizes, however, this can be reported in most cases with extreme caution. Your data analyst will advise you.

2. It appears that Program A is the best program for open-structured classrooms, but either Program A or Program C is best for traditional classrooms. If you have unequal cell sizes, however, you will need to use great caution in reporting any findings other than this interaction. Consult your data analyst.

For the sake of completeness, you should follow up an analysis when an ANOVA has shown significance by having the data analyst check whether the difference between *any single pair* of programs is significant. This analysis is called a *post hoc comparison.* Post hoc comparison is necessary because the ANOVA only tells you that a significant difference is likely to be found *somewhere* in the data. It doesn't tell you *which* differences are significant. An ANOVA might show significant program effects with, for example, these cell means:

Example

TABLE J
Cell Means for Classrooms

	Program A	Program B	Program C
open structured	72	61	59
traditional structured	70	62	58

It may well be that the difference between Programs B and C is *not* significant; but Program A is significantly different from C or perhaps from both B and C.

In general, when dealing with ANOVA results, remember that judgments about which program is superior should not rely on one single set of results. Be careful, as well, not to place too much faith in small differences, and remember that the ANOVA says there is a significant difference somewhere in the data, but it does not tell where.

Summary

Below is a step-by-step summary of a procedure for setting up and analyzing an analysis of variance (ANOVA) design. The design here compares two factors: Factor 1 has four levels (e.g., four versions of an experimental training program); Factor 2 has three levels (e.g., work sites of three different sizes).

1. Write down the factors on two sides of a box:

Factor 1

Factor 2

2. Fill in the levels of each factor and thus divide the box into cells. This example has a 4-by-3 design:

Factor 1

		level 1	level 2	level 3	level 4
Factor 2	1				
	2				
	3				

3. Assign or find cases for each of the cells; try to keep all sizes equal. The cases may be individuals, training classrooms, or work sites.
4. Collect scores on the outcome measure for all the cases in each cell.
5. Give the data to the data analyst, asking for an analysis of variance (ANOVA) to test the significance of the effects of the factors and the significance of interactions. Be sure to tell her that you want to have a table of cell means as well as an ANOVA table.
6. When the data return, prepare a graph with the possible cell means from the outcome measure listed along the vertical axis and the levels of one factor on the horizontal axis.

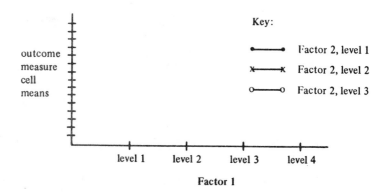

Graph the scores for Factor 2 according to the key.

7. Examine the ANOVA table. First check the *interaction row*. Is the F value significant? If so, there are probably significant differences between one factor's results depending upon what level of the other factor you examine. Exercising proper caution where there are unequal cell sizes, check the graph of the cell means and report the program effects (Factor 1) separately for each level of Factor 2 (work site size). If the interaction "F" is *not* significant, then check for main effects—effects which are the same no matter what the level of the other factor—and report these.
8. Since the ANOVA has probably left you doubtful about which *pairs* of cell means are significantly different, ask the data analyst to do *post hoc comparisons.*

For Further Reading

Glass, G. V, & Stanley, J. C. (1970). *Statistical methods in education and psychology.* Englewood Cliffs, NJ: Prentice-Hall.

Iverson, G., & Norpoth, H. (1987). *Analysis of variance* (2nd ed.). Newbury Park, CA: Sage.

Chapter 8

How to Randomize

Randomization will be useful to you any time you want to assure *sameness* or *representativeness* of assignment or selection. Several of the evaluation designs discussed in this book depend on random assignment of students or classes to programs. Randomization of assignment allows you to assume that groups to whom different programs will be given are initially alike.[1] Knowing this helps you draw logical conclusions about the *causes* of the results that you eventually measure.

Often you might want a small group of students to represent a larger one. Adequate representation can best be ensured by random *selection* of representatives from the larger group.

This chapter gives step-by-step directions for both (1) random *assignment* of a whole population of individuals or classes to two or more groups, and (2) random *selection* of a small but maximally representative sample from a large group. Before you go about assigning and selecting, though, it is important that you devote some attention to the problem of what units—individuals, teams, classrooms, schools, or work sites—will be randomized in your situation.

The Unit of Analysis Problem

You will have noticed that during discussion of the designs which call for randomization—Designs 1 and 2—examples included the randomization of individuals or groups of individuals such as classes, schools, and work sites. The choice of *which* of these "units" to randomize belongs to the evaluator, although in many situations practical constraints will limit the alternatives. Your decision about which units will be randomized affects the interpretation of your results and is usually referred to as *the unit of analysis problem.*

The first step in identifying the proper unit of analysis in your situation is to ask yourself:

What general statements will be made from the information collected? Will it be about individuals or some groups of individuals?

Of course, all programs ultimately wish to make an impact upon the individual. But they might attempt to do this by aiming a major change at some other level—by retraining *managers*, perhaps, or integrating *schools*. An individualized learning program, for instance, alters school practice at the *student* level. Materials are provided which students use individually, and presumably each student is treated differently. If you wish to use an evaluation of an individualized program to make statements about program impact on certain *kinds of students* or to recommend changes in the program for students of a particular type, then the unit of analysis for your study is clearly the student. If, on the other hand, you want to evaluate whether installing an individualized program has worked *at all*—by raising a general level of achievement, then your unit of analysis is more appropriately the *classroom* or even perhaps the *school*. As you can see, choice of appropriate unit is relative: *The correct unit of analysis will usually be the one about which your evaluation will make recommendations.*

Generally, school and work programs focus on *groups*. This is the case with the introduction of new textbooks or new equipment, changes in organizational structure or scheduling, provision of classroom aides, introduction of nutrition, health, or benefit programs, and so forth. Management in-service programs, for instance, aim at affecting individual employee performance by means of changes made in the *manager's* behavior. In such cases, the unit of analysis should most often be the department or manager's work group. This is because the effect of the intervention is expected to be *diffused* among the group showing an overall change in the entire group rather than a specific change among certain sorts of individuals. What is more, suggestions based on the evaluation will likely be applied to the whole group, affecting all its members as a unit.

Of course, programs can aim at impact on the school, district, or entire work site as well. Programs which focus on changing the attitudes or behavior of the *principal* or which alter the physical setting or population characteristics of a school suggest a unit of analysis at the building level. Similarly, some federal or state programs initiate innovations aimed at the school district. If the results of evaluations of these programs will influence policy only about what the government requires districts to do and *not* what districts require schools to do, then the correct unit of analysis is the district. As evaluator, you might want, of course, to make additional statements about the impact of a districtwide program upon schools for the use of people in the district office. But if the government is your prime sponsor, you must first attend to the major evaluation question:

What impact did this districtwide program have on the district as a whole?

Now, why does assuring that an evaluation focus on the proper unit of analysis present a *problem?* The section of this book dealing with analysis of results from randomized designs, you will remember, mentioned that the *number of cases* within a random sample affects the strength of the conclusions which can be drawn from an evaluation study. Randomization with few units per group is *unlikely* to achieve experimental and control groups which are initially equivalent; and if a case for initial equality of groups cannot be supported, then outcome findings cannot be attributed solely to the program or treatment. The unit of analysis *problem* arises from the practical fact that larger units of analysis, such as classrooms, schools, and districts, usually exist in numbers too small to ensure establishment of equal groups through randomization. With limited numbers of cases, simple random assignment may produce groups that are quite different from one another. For example, suppose six schools have consistently produced the following average percentiles in reading comprehension:

Jefferson	92
Duquesne	50
Austin	61
Washington	43
Hamilton	90
Johnson	79

Simple random assignment to two groups might put Hamilton, Johnson and Jefferson in the same group. This would make the two groups uneven—one with reading achievement at the 92nd, 90th, and 79th percentiles, and another with average percentile scores of 50, 61, and 43. You see that the smaller the number of schools to be randomly assigned, the more likely it is that you will encounter problems of this sort.

Besides the high probability of initial inequality of small groups, the unit of analysis problem has another facet. Small numbers make some statistical analyses impossible, and where analysis *can* be performed small samples reduce the likelihood that even fairly substantial differences will be statistically significant. This is because statistical tests take into account the size of the groups producing the means being compared when determining significance. The smaller the group, the less likely it is that the mean produced actually reflects the mean that it is supposed to represent—the mean, for instance, of all classrooms which could conceivably use the particular program. Because your means from small samples are likely to be "off," statistical tests will demand a very large difference between the means you obtain before they bestow significance.

The unit of analysis problem can be most deftly dealt with by following a few rules of thumb:

1. *Try to achieve random assignment with the smallest unit possible,* even when your major analysis will focus at a larger level. If you are conducting an evaluation of a teacher in-service program, for instance,

where the primary target of the program is the teacher, the unit of analysis will be the classroom. If you plan to measure the effect of this program on class achievement or attitudes, you will report, say, an average for the *group* of classrooms whose teachers participated in a particular program. In this situation, you will boost the credibility of your results if you try to randomly assign *students, as well as teachers,* to classrooms. This will support the notion that all the classrooms participating in the study were initially alike. In addition, randomizing students will reduce the *variability* among classes receiving the *same* program—something to which the statistical test also attends. If all classes receiving Program X produce roughly the same mean scores, the chance is increased that the mean for the *group* of all Program X classrooms will be statistically different from the mean for Program C. Of course, if there are *many* teachers—60 perhaps—then assigning teachers to intact classrooms without attention to classroom composition itself might still allow a credible study. Randomizing 60 classrooms to two treatments should yield fairly equal groups. With smaller numbers, though, your audience will need to know that the classrooms were initially equivalent—or that some care has been taken to equally distribute unusual classes to the two groups. The best designs, you will note, are randomized throughout. In actual settings, however, these are practically impossible to achieve.

2. *If you cannot randomize at a smaller level than the unit of analysis on which you must focus, then try to work with as many of these units as possible.* If the program will be delivered to only four schools or four branch offices of a company, then try to influence *which* schools or branches and urge strongly that they be randomly chosen. You then can compare the four randomly chosen schools or branches with four others, although generalizing from a sample size of four will be difficult.

3. *Try to use blocked randomization.* The basic blocking procedure is discussed at length on pages 153 and 154. Essentially, blocking directs you first to classify the units available for randomization according to a characteristic that is likely to affect the outcome of the evaluation, and then randomly to assign units from each block to the groups you are forming. For instance, in the randomization of schools example mentioned above, since overall average percentiles are available, schools can be blocked before random formation of an experimental and control group. Jefferson and Hamilton Schools, for instance, would form one block on the basis of their higher achievement records. If you are evaluating a program to decrease employee turnover in a very large company, branch offices might be blocked according to past turnover rates. The branches from each of the high and low turnover rate blocks could be randomly assigned to the experimental and control groups. This process ensures better equivalence between the two groups formed than does simple randomization.

4. *Try to build a case that the intact, already constituted groups which you must randomize are sufficiently equivalent such that they might as well have been randomly composed.* You might, for instance, find yourself in the common situation of evaluating a program for which the classroom is the proper unit of focus. But there are very few of these; so few that assigning them randomly to programs will not ensure initially equivalent E- and C-groups. And the ideal solution, random distribution of students among the classes, will not be possible. The next best solution is to examine carefully the characteristics of students in each class and the process by which they were assigned to classes. If you can argue that no particular plan placed students in one class or the other, and that it is hard to tell the composition of one classroom from another—students seem of equal background, of equal ability, and teachers seem equal in commitment, motivation, and instructional style—then you can build the case that the classes are so alike that they *might have been* randomly composed. What is more, if all classrooms do not look alike, perhaps groups of them do, and you can use these groups as a basis for blocked randomization. As with any instance when you can defend the initial equality of experimental and control groups, a case for apparent randomness will lend credibility to your eventual conclusions.

5. *Keep the implementation of the programs faithful to plan so that if a large difference between their effectiveness is to be found, it will occur.* Try to ensure that both programs are running at their best and strongest. By all means, keep them from intermingling and contaminating one another.

Random Assignment of Students,
Classrooms, or Schools to Programs

An assignment is random if each case—individual or group—has an equal chance to be chosen. By definition, random assignment is fair and unbiased—a point to bear in mind if you have difficulty persuading people to go along with randomization.

Simple Random Assignment

Simple random assignment is appropriate when large numbers are to be randomized. There are at least four ways to achieve simple random assignment of a pool of individuals or groups to programs. Which method is best to use depends on the situation where randomization is needed:

1. *Coin toss.* Suppose individuals are to be randomly assigned to one of *two* programs. You could prepare a list of all eligible people, then toss

a coin for each one in turn, providing it's a fair coin: "Heads you go to Program X, tails you go to Program C." But if individuals are to be randomly assigned to *three* groups, the coin-tossing procedure will be cumbersome. And, since tossing coins takes a considerable amount of time, it is impractical in most instances.

2. *Random number tables.* Researchers often use random number tables. These are listed at the back of many statistics books. Random number tables are usually generated by computers and consist of lists of the numerals 0 through 9 that are truly random. They are useful for every randomization situation, but they too have proven somewhat cumbersome in actual practice.

3. *Deck of cards.* You can make yourself a "Handy Randomizing Deck" (HRD) by numbering 75 playing cards "1" through "75" with a black magic marker. Seventy-five cards are suggested since this number will cover most randomization situations you encounter but still provide a deck that can be easily shuffled. The HRD makes procedures for random assignment clearly comprehensible and easy to achieve. Each card can represent a person to be assigned to a program—or an item to be given on a test—or whatever is to be randomly assigned or selected. Pages 142 and 145 give directions for various randomization procedures using the HRD.

4. *A prepared list.* Table 8, pages 151 and 152 of this chapter, is entitled "Roster for Random Assignment to 2, 3, 4 or 5 Groups." The table is composed of lists prepared by computer-generated randomization. To use Table 8 to form, say, 4 groups, just write individuals' names alphabetically on the roster and read off, from the "4 group" column the number of the group to which each student is assigned. A procedure for using Table 8 is outlined in greater detail on pages 149-150.

All of these procedures accomplish *simple* randomization. They attempt to form roughly equivalent groups from a collection of individuals or groups about whom nothing—at least nothing likely to affect program outcomes—is known. When critical characteristics *are* known, they should be used to even further ensure equivalence of groups formed through random assignment. Both *blocking* and *matching*, whose descriptions begin on page 150, do this by ensuring equal distribution of important factors—such as high IQ.

The following section describes three procedures for *simple* randomization. Simple randomization is just that—no particular characteristics of the students to be assigned are taken into account beforehand. The procedures will ensure roughly equivalent groups, particularly where large numbers (more than 30 per group) are involved. They represent good methods for randomization which few skeptics will question.

**Step-by-step instructions for using the
handy randomizing deck (HRD)
for simple random assignment**

The HRD randomization method described below concerns assignment of *individuals*. It can also be applied when assigning groups to programs or when assigning objectives or items to test forms. The list described in step 1 could then be a list of classes (by teacher's name or room number, etc.), a list of work sites, or a list of objectives or items identified by number.

Suppose 49 students are to be assigned randomly to three reading programs, X, Y, and Z.

1. List the 49 students alphabetically. Any order which is convenient will do, but keeping alphabetical lists is usually most efficient. Number each name on the list "1" through "49."

2. Pull cards "1" through "49" from the HRD.

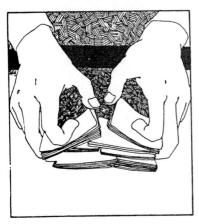

3. Shuffle the 49 cards thoroughly. Shuffle and cut several times.

4. Deal the 49 cards into three piles, one for Program X, one for Y, and one for Z. (Put card-sized squares marked X, Y, and Z on paper if necessary.) Deal a card to X, one to Y, one to Z, and repeat until all 49 cards have been dealt. One group will turn out to have one more student than the others. This is OK.

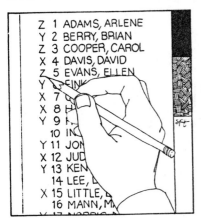

5. Take the pile of cards for Program X. Look at the number on the first card and write an X next to the name of the student with the number on the list. Continue marking X's for all students whose numbers are in the X pile. Take the pile for Program Y and mark Y's next to these students. Do the same for pile Z.

PROGRAM X	PROGRAM Y	PROGRAM Z
DAVIS, D.	BERRY, B.	ADAMS, A.
GARDEN, G.	FINK, F.	COOPER, C.
HANDLER, H.	HUNT. H.	EVANS, E.
JUDSEN, J.	JONES, J.	INGLIS, I.
LITTLE, L	KENDALL, K.	LEE, L.
RYAN, R.	NORRIS, N.	MANN, M.
SANFORD, S.	OLSEN, O.	PERRY, P.
WESTON, W.	POTTS, P.	THOMAS, T.
WILCOX, W.	TOWNS, T.	TURNER, T.

6. Have your annotated list typed into three separate lists of the students in each program. If your original list was alphabetized, the three lists can easily be typed alphabetically.

This procedure can be used regardless of the number of groups or individuals to be assigned. If you have *more than* 75 students to be assigned to groups, use this simple extension of the procedure:

Do the randomization as described for the first 75 students. Then, using the list of students from the 76th one on, start again at 1 to number the students. Select as many cards as you need to represent the remaining students. (If you have 125 students in all, you will use cards numbered "1" to "50.") Make sure, when you are finished, that the number of students you have assigned to each program is roughly the same. Doing the randomization in two (or more) phases like this *will* produce adequate random assignment.

Simple random assignment with the HRD conducted in public

Sometimes it is necessary or desirable to make the random assignment procedure public. For example, if a department is to be divided into two or more groups, the head of the department might want the employees to realize that the groups are made up randomly. Knowing this will avoid suspicions of favoritism or a feeling of having been specially chosen. Both of these might influence results.

Here is a suggested method:

1. Have the employees to be assigned to groups assemble in one room. Give each a numbered file card (numbered according to how many employees you have) on which to write his name and whatever other information you may need.

2. Explain the need for randomization. You might be able to point out that lack of an adequate supply of materials makes random assignment necessary or that you really have no idea which of the programs to which people will be assigned is best. Each program is something new, and only the results will show which is most effective.

3. Select as many HRD cards as you have employees. The numbers should correspond to the numbered file cards in the employees' possession.

4. Shuffle the HRD cards and deal them into as many piles as there are programs. Everyone should be able to see the shuffling and dealing. In fact, you might want to have an employee do this just to allay fears of "stacking the deck."

5. Pick up the first pile of HRD cards and read out the numbers. Employees who have these numbers on their file cards should turn them in. A list of each program's members should then be completed.

**Step-by-step instructions for using
the prepared random number list
for simple random assignment**

Like the HRD procedures, the randomization method described below concerns assignment of *individuals*. It can also be applied when assigning groups to programs or when assigning items or objectives to test forms. The list described in step 1 would then be a list of classes (by teacher's name or room number, etc.), a list of work sites, or a list of objectives or items identified by number.

Suppose 49 students are to be assigned randomly to three reading programs, X, Y, and Z.

1. Make a copy of pages 151 and 152 of this book—Table 8, the *Roster for Random Assignment to 2, 3, 4, or 5 Groups.*

2. In the left-hand column, list in alphabetical order the names of *all* the students.

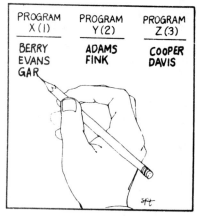

STUDENT NAME	2 GROUPS	3 GROUPS
1 ADAMS, ARLENE	2	2
2 BERRY, BRIAN	1	1
3 COOPER, CAROL	1	3
4 DAVIS, DAVID	2	3
5 EVANS, ELLEN	1	1
6 FINK, FRED	2	2
7 GARDEN, GRAHAM	2	1
8 H	1	2
	1	3
	2	3
	1	2
	2	1
	1	2
	2	1
	1	3

3. Decide how many groups you wish to form, corresponding to the number of alternative programs you wish to compare—3, in this case—and circle this column lengthwise.

PROGRAM X (1)	PROGRAM Y (2)	PROGRAM Z (3)
BERRY	ADAMS	COOPER
EVANS	FINK	DAVIS
GAR		

4. Look at the number which corresponds to each name and make a new list of the students assigned to each group. These are the random groups.

More Credible **Random Assignment**: Blocking and Matching

Blocking

Blocking or blocked randomization is the method of choice when the number of units to be randomized is small. It allows you to seek out those features of individuals that might affect program results and make sure that they are distributed equally in the groups you construct.

Blocking is so called because it requires that individuals (or groups, whichever is to be assigned) be listed in *blocks* before randomization takes place. There might be, for example, blocks of females and males of high and low ability groups. Blocks can reflect whatever factor is likely to affect performance in the program. Then the E-group and C-group are formed by random assignment from each block.

TABLE 8
Roster for Random Assignment to 2, 3, 4, or 5 Groups

Individual's Name	2 Groups	3 Groups	4 Groups	5 Groups
1	2	2	4	3
2	1	1	1	5
3	1	3	2	2
4	2	3	3	1
5	1	1	1	4
6	2	2	4	2
7	2	1	3	1
8	1	2	2	3
9	1	3	3	5
10	2	3	4	4
11	1	2	2	1
12	2	1	1	4
13	1	2	2	3
14	2	1	3	5
15	2	3	4	2
16	1	1	1	3
17	2	3	1	1
18	1	2	3	2
19	2	3	2	5
20	1	2	4	4
21	2	1	2	1
22	1	2	3	2
23	1	3	4	3
24	2	1	1	5
25	1	3	3	4
26	1	2	1	3
27	2	1	2	1
28	2	1	4	5
29	2	2	3	4
30	1	3	4	2
31	1	2	2	5
32	2	1	1	4
33	1	3	2	2
34	1	2	3	3
35	2	3	1	1
36	2	1	4	5
37	2	3	1	1
38	1	2	4	2
39	2	1	2	3
40	1	1	3	4

TABLE 8 (continued)

Individual's Name	2 Groups	3 Groups	4 Groups	5 Groups
41	2	2	4	5
42	1	3	2	4
43	2	3	3	2
44	1	1	1	1
45	2	2	2	3
46	2	3	1	4
47	1	2	4	3
48	1	1	3	5
49	1	3	1	2
50	2	1	3	1
51	1	2	4	3
52	2	1	2	2
53	1	3	4	4
54	2	2	1	1
55	1	1	2	5
56	2	3	3	2
57	1	2	2	4
58	2	1	3	5
59	2	2	4	3
60	1	3	1	1
61	1	2	1	1
62	1	1	2	3
63	2	3	3	5
64	2	1	4	2
65	1	3	1	4
66	1	2	3	3
67	2	2	4	1
68	2	3	2	4
69	2	1	2	5
70	1	1	4	2
71	1	3	1	2
72	2	2	3	4
73	2	3	4	5
74	1	1	3	3
75	2	2	2	1
76	1	2	1	2
77	2	3	2	3
78	2	1	4	1
79	1	1	3	4
80	1	2	1	5

Blocking can give you a great deal of information about the different effects that the program has on people with various blocked characteristics. This could affect the ambitiousness of the statistical analyses you perform. If your measurement plans were determined by Designs 1, 2, or 3, and you used random sampling, then the analysis you would use is the t-test. If you used blocking in your random assignment, however, and your groups are large enough, then your design has the power to provide you with more detailed information about the program's effects. Should you have enough cases, you can use an analysis of variance (ANOVA), discussed in Chapter 7. If you use ANOVA, then the sample size discussion on pages 161 to 162 applies to *each* subgroup represented (that is, to each characteristic represented by a cell in the ANOVA matrix). Because of these sample size requirements, analysis of variance requires larger groups. In evaluations, analysis by subgroups will be desirable only when required or when you have an inescapably strong hunch that a certain characteristic will differentially affect results.

A standard blocking procedure

The basic blocking procedure is a little more complex than simple randomization. This section presents a step-by-step outline of the standard blocking procedure. To detail the procedure, focus is on the frequent situation of blocking individuals by sex. You may, of course, wish to block any number of other characteristics. Alter the procedure to your needs, but follow the basic steps outlined below:

1. Decide on the feature you wish to use for blocking—IQ, math achievement, reading proficiency, and so on. This will be the feature that you feel might itself cause differential results from completing programs if it were not equally distributed between the groups. If, for instance, your new program concerns math, you may want to make sure that you evenly distribute prior math achievement. You might want to block according to *more than one* feature, say sex *and* math ability *and* family educational background. This is generally a good idea if you have enough people or classes to go around; it assures even more equivalent groups. In this case—three features—you will need at least eight blocks (two levels of each of three features) from which to assign.

2. Find a measure of the feature(s) that has been, or could be, administered to individuals. This measure will form the basis for blocking. Again, if you want to equalize math achievement, use math achievement test scores or last year's math grade averages as the basis for blocking. By the same token, if you want the groups to be equal in general ability, use IQ scores. If you have no measure available at all and cannot administer one, then have teachers or supervisors rank

individuals in order according to informal assessment of the degree to which each individual possesses the characteristic.

3. Administer the measure if you find that you do not already have the results you need.

4. *List the individuals in the order* in which they score on the blocking measure.

5. Decide how many "blocks" you wish to construct based on this feature. Sex, for example, obviously provides you with only two categories, but IQ could yield three or more blocks: LOW, MEDIUM and HIGH; or LOW, SLIGHTLY BELOW AVERAGE, SLIGHTLY ABOVE AVERAGE, and HIGH, and so on. For *continuous* measures, such as IQ, achievement, and SES, *you* will have to decide the number of categories for blocking. In general, you should keep the number of blocks down to no more than three or four. Choose the number of categories and cut-off scores that seem to give you similar kinds of individuals in each block. If the scores seem fairly well spread, select three or four categories.

6. Using the cut-off scores you've chosen, divide the list into the number of blocks you've decided to use.

7. Use a method for simple random assignment to place individuals *from each block* into the treatment groups.

Matched pairs

If individuals are to be assigned to an E-group and a C-group, one could go to the extreme of creating so many blocks that only two people were left in each. This extreme is actually a good idea. It is the method of *matched pairs.* From these pairs of people who are equal in some crucial characteristics, one member is assigned to the E-group and one to the C-group.

The matched-pairs procedure is especially useful if you are evaluating a *short-term program* or conducting a small experiment. These are likely to show only a small difference in results between the experimental (Program X) and control groups (Program C). Matching makes the differing groups receiving each program as initially alike as possible and yields a powerful design. The rigorous but highly credible "matched group t-test" is employed to test the significance of differences in results. The matched pairs procedure is recommended for use only when *people* are to be assigned randomly. *Groups* of people, even classrooms, cannot be alike enough to warrant matching.

Making matched pairs might not be such a good idea for evaluating programs that will run for a long time—say, a whole school year. The reason for this is the problem of *attrition*—individuals dropping out or having long absences over the course of the program. The statistical analysis for matched pairs depends on both members of the pair completing the program. When one pair member drops out or is absent excessively, the other pair member's data must also be deleted. This is why using matched pairs is not useful when evaluating a long-term program: it means running the risk of losing data for a great many individuals since dropouts and absences tend to increase over the long haul. If the number of people receiving each program is small at the outset, the risk becomes enormous. In addition, you must remember the major reason for using matched pairs is to maximize the likelihood of obtaining statistical significance from a small effect. A program that runs six weeks or more will probably show a fairly sizable effect, thus eliminating a need for such careful matching.

Step-by-step instructions for forming E- and C-groups from matched pairs

1. Collect the individuals' scores on an appropriate measure and list them in rank order writing each person's name in order from highest to lowest. The most appropriate measure to use as a basis for matching is one that best predicts final results, for instance, a math achievement pretest for a math program.

2. Make matched pairs: Circle pairs of people who are adjacent on the list. Since exact matches of pairs of people cannot be achieved, this procedure simply produces the closest possible pairs. If there is an odd number of people, one name should be chosen at random from the list and excluded from the analysis. The person can still, of course, receive the program.

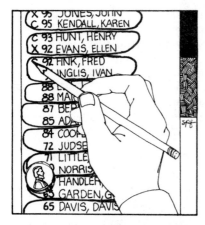

3. Since you are constructing two groups, you can use a coin toss for random assignment. For each pair, toss the coin once. Decide which is tails–Program X for example–then make the toss for the first person listed in the pair. If the toss comes out tails, write an "X" next to the first person's name. If it's heads, mark a "C" next to the name. Assign the other member of the pair to the other program.

4. Have separate lists of the people in each program typed.

**The Borderline Method of Forming
a True Control Group in Special Programs**

When a group of individuals is to be selected for a remedial program, the most needy are generally clearly identifiable. Their scores on relevant tests are invariably the lowest, or there is complete agreement among their supervisors or teachers that they are the worst. However, as you near the cutoff point, the decisions you have to make are usually less distinct. For example, John scored higher than David on the last test, but usually he scores lower. Which person should be put in the program if there is not room for both?

This indecision is quite justifiable. Tests are not perfect measurements. There is often error in test scores, and therefore *fine* distinctions cannot be made. John may have scored 34 whereas David scored 32, but David might still be better. However, you must consider Michael, who, scoring 21, is clearly in need of the program.

Thus, when planners set out to select those in need of a program, they must choose from among a large group of students those who are *clearly* in need, and decide from among a *borderline group*[2] who should and who should not be in the program.

Drawing on this information you can design a good evaluation of a compensatory or remedial program that is still fair to all concerned. This needed and valuable evaluation of a remedial program can be done by focusing on the *borderline* individuals. While the neediest ones *all* receive the program, a Program X group and a true control group can be formed from the *borderline* group. Suppose a remedial reading class has room for 28 students. The 20 worst readers are placed in the program. The next 16 students form the borderline group. A random selection of 8 of these students is placed in the program; the other 8 do not go into the remedial program. Figure 4 illustrates how a distribution of reading scores can be used to identify the most needy and borderline groups.

Random assignment of part of the students from the borderline group to the new program (X) and part to a comparison or control group (C) will allow you to test the relative effectiveness of your new program *without neglecting the group of children who you feel most morally bound to help*. These most needy students will receive the program, but they will not take part in the evaluation study.

This design method is an excellent—and innovative—way to test the value of special programs. It is vastly preferable to the simple Before-and-After Design. It eliminates the problems of data interpretation that result from regression effects. These are problems which plague the Before-and-After Design whenever a program is given to individuals with initially extreme scores.

It is important to recognize one characteristic of the borderline method: it produces results that are, strictly speaking, generalizable only to borderline groups. For example, it is evident that if the evaluation shows that borderline students who received the program outscored borderline students who did not receive it, the generalization that can be made is that the program is beneficial *for borderline students*. The effect of the program on the most needy students cannot necessarily be inferred from its tested effects on the borderline students who formed the experimental and control groups.

Yet this very limitation of the borderline method can sometimes be a great virtue. It has specific bearing on cases where the decision about a program is not whether to drop it or continue it, but rather whether to expand it to include more people. Should the school, for example, set up two remedial reading classes rather than just one? If your evaluation has used a borderline control group and has shown that the program is beneficial for borderline students, you are in the strongest possible position to recommend expansion of the program to include more such students.

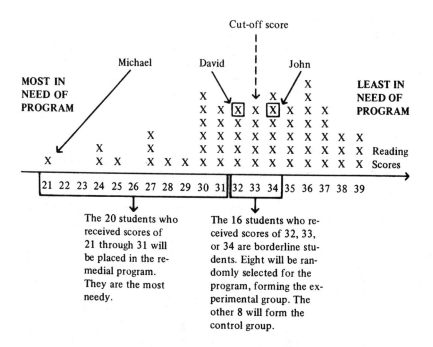

Figure 4. How a plot of reading scores is used (1) to assign the most in need to a remedial program and (2) to form an experimental group and control group out of borderline students.

Unfortunately, the political surround of many compensatory education programs might prohibit use of the borderline method. In order to receive funds, you might be strictly required to give the program to *all* students falling below the cut-off score. If this is the case, and you can find no way to randomize student assignment to programs, then consider using a cluster of students scoring *above but near* the cut-off score as a nonequivalent control group. Compare their posttest scores with an equal number of students who fell just *below* the cut-off score and therefore received the program. This solution is not nearly so satisfactory as the borderline method described here, but it will allow you to make at least an informal assessment of program results: the "borderline" students who squeezed into the program should be performing at least as well as the controls.

Step-by-step instructions for forming a borderline control group

1. Obtain scores on a test relevant to the new program for all individuals who might possibly take part in it. These scores might be the results of an objective test or they might be teacher ratings.

2. Graph these scores and label the two ends "most in need of the program" and "least in need." A remedial program will have the lowest scores marked "most in need"; a program for gifted children would have the highest scores marked "most in need."

3. Decide how many individuals can be placed in the program.

4. Count off this number from the "most in need" end of the distribution, and mark the score where this brings you (use an arrow). If you were simply using

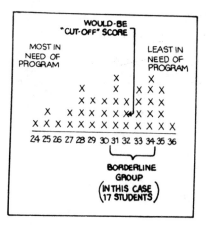

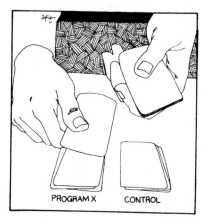

this distribution to assign individuals to the program, the arrow would be marking the cut-off score. But you now need to form a borderline group around the cut-off score.

5. Count out at least six people *at and on each side* of the cut-off score. The 12 or more people you have counted (six on each side—plus any who have the same score as the sixth person on each side) form the borderline group.

6. Make a numbered list of the borderline group.

7. Use a coin toss, the HRD, or the Prepared Random Number List method to randomly assign half the people on the list to the program and the other half to the control group.

Alternatively, put the borderline group names in a hat or other receptacle, shake, and draw out half the names for the program.

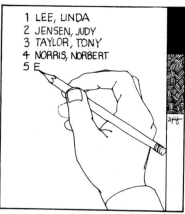

Selecting a Random Sample

There may be occasions when you need to select a random *sample* from a large number of people or groups, or a sample of items or objectives from a larger pool. This situation will be slightly different from those in which you need to randomly *assign* all of the people, or items, or whatever to programs. For example, you may wish to interview employees in a special program but have insufficient time to talk to everyone. Depending upon the time you have available for interviewing and the number of employees in the program, you may decide to interview as few as 10% or as many as 25% of the people involved. Another situation in which you might need a sample of people is when using a Time Series Design (Designs 4 and 5) where you wish to poll a random sample of people in a school or work site.

Deciding on the *size* of the sample will be the first necessary step. Here one rule-of-thumb best applies: make the sample as large as you can afford in terms of time and money. A large sample best represents the whole group; the smaller it becomes, the less you can expect its outcomes to reflect accurately what you would have obtained by testing everyone. Generally, for performing statistical analyses, a sample size of 30 is considered adequate for gaining a stable measure no matter what the size of the group being represented. It goes without saying that whatever the size of the sample, you must take care to ensure that it adequately *represents* the range of actual opinions or abilities in the larger population.

Considerable writing and discussion have been spent on the issue of sample size. Some general principles have emerged, and though they are not unanimously sanctioned, they are passed on to you here: if you wish to use the results gained from the sample to make a *general statement* about all people having a certain characteristic or who are likely to take part in a certain program—in other words, if the population you wish to generalize to is essentially infinite—then *ask* yourself and knowledgeable others for opinions. Consider the credibility to your audience of various sized samples. Ask yourself:

What size sample would I insist upon before I believed the results of research that proposed to make general statements about all people with characteristic X?

Ask your colleagues and your own evaluation audience. Since the provision of credible information is your ultimate responsibility in doing the evaluation, use people's judgments to help you decide on an adequate sample size. What's more, what you find from this survey may surprise you: a lot of people refuse to believe anything based on a sample.

More usually in evaluation situations, the population of people about whom you wish to make a statement is easily described and counted. It is *finite*, such as the population of parents at a particular junior high, or the salespeople in a certain department store. For these situations, researchers have determined, via a complex formula, the sample sizes necessary for credible representation of finite groups.

Table 9 is provided here as a handy guide for deciding the necessary size of your sample. Simply set "N" at the size of the *whole group* (population) which the sample is to represent, and note the corresponding "s." This is the suggested sample size. If you can match the suggested size, you can be fairly certain of accurate representation through simple random sampling. If you cannot obtain one that large, consider your results less credible unless you can randomize through stratification.

The critical concern in using samples to represent larger groups is, of course, the problem of ensuring accurate representation. Adequate sample size helps increase representativeness. So does *stratifying*. Stratifying requires that you select *separately* from among groups of people who differ according to some critical characteristic(s) which might affect your results—such as age, sex, or IQ. The *whole* sample selected should therefore represent various subgroups in the proportions to which they contribute to the larger group.

If you do decide to stratify, then use the directions for selecting a simple random sample over and over again for each subgroup. In performing step 1, make separate lists of people for each characteristic to be separately sampled, and repeat steps 2 through 5 for each subgroup sample to be drawn.

Using a List to Select a Random Sample

The method described below for selecting a random sample of *students* can also be used when selecting samples of other individuals or groups, or when selecting test items from a larger item pool—any time you need to reduce the number of units with which you must work while ensuring the representativeness of those selected for your study.

STUDENT
1   ADAMS, ARLENE
2   BERRY, BRIAN
3   COOPER, CAROL
4   DAVIS, DAVID

1. Make or obtain a numbered list of the whole available group. Any order that is not based on grouping by critical characteristics will do. Alphabetical order will work fine.

TABLE 9
Table for Determining Sample Size from a Given Population

N	s	N	s	N	s
10	10	220	140	1200	291
15	14	230	144	1300	297
20	19	240	148	1400	302
25	24	250	152	1500	306
30	28	260	155	1600	310
35	32	270	159	1700	313
40	36	280	162	1800	317
45	40	290	165	1900	320
50	44	300	169	2000	322
55	48	320	175	2200	327
60	52	340	181	2400	331
65	56	360	186	2600	335
70	59	380	191	2800	338
75	63	400	196	3000	341
80	66	420	201	3500	346
85	70	440	205	4000	351
90	73	460	210	4500	354
95	76	480	214	5000	357
100	80	500	217	6000	361
110	86	550	228	7000	364
120	92	600	234	8000	367
130	97	650	242	9000	368
140	103	700	248	10000	370
150	106	750	254	15000	375
160	113	800	260	20000	377
170	118	850	265	30000	379
180	123	900	269	40000	380
190	127	950	274	50000	381
200	133	1000	278	75000	382
210	136	1100	285	100000	384

SOURCE: Krijcie, R. V., & Morgan, D. W. (1970). This table was based on a formula published by the research division of the National Education Association.
NOTE: N is population size; s is sample size.

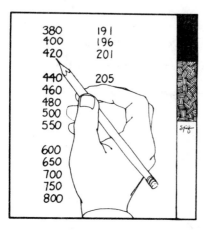

2. Use Table 9, p. 163, or the suggestions on p. 161, tempered by the practical constraints of your situation, to decide upon a sample size, s.

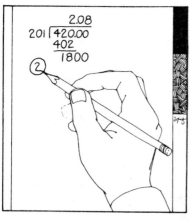

3. Divide N, the size of the whole available group, by s. Round either up or down, that is, change decimals to the next whole number.

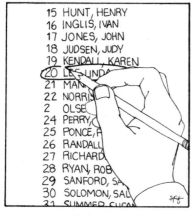

4. Use this whole number to count down the list and circle selected people. If the number is 2, for instance, then circle and select every second name.

5. Make a list of the people who have been chosen.

NOTES

1. Similarly, if you want to construct two tests (say, to use as a pretest and posttest) from a pool of only slightly different items that measure the same skills, you can ensure adequately similar tests by randomly assigning items from a large pool to the two test forms. These are technically called "content equivalent forms." Though all the examples in this chapter refer to assignment and selection of *people*, randomization procedures are general and can be applied as effectively in more mundane situations, such as the assignment of items to tests or the selection of dates when observers will examine a classroom.

2. Psychometricians would precisely define the borderline group by using the *standard error of measurement* of the test, but this is not necessary for the purposes of this book.

For Further Reading

Cochran, W. G. (1953). *Sampling techniques.* New York: John Wiley.

Sudman, S. (1976). *Applied sampling.* New York: Academic Press.

References

Alkin, M. C., Kosecoff, J., Fitz-Gibbon, C., & Seligman, R. (1974). *Evaluation and decision making: The Title VII experience* (CSE Monograph Series in Evaluation no. 4). Los Angeles: Center for the Study of Evaluation.

Ball, S., & Bogatz, G. A. (1970). *The first year of Sesame Street: An evaluation.* Princeton, NJ: Educational Testing Service.

Campbell, D. T., & Stanley, J. C. (1966). *Experimental and quasi-experimental designs for research.* Chicago: Rand McNally.

Cooke, T. D., and Campbell, D. T. (1976). The design and conduct of quasi-experimental and true experiments in field settings. In M. Dunnette (Ed.), *Handbook of industrial and organizational psychology.* Chicago: Rand McNally College Publishing.

Cooke, T. D. et al. (1975). *Sesame Street revisited.* New York: Russell Sage Foundation.

Foat, C. M. (1974). *Selecting exemplary compensation education projects for dissemination via project information packages* (tech. rep. no. UR-242). Los Altos, CA: RMC Research Corporation.

Glass, G. V, & Stanley, J. C. (1970). *Statistical methods in education and psychology.* Englewood Cliffs, NJ: Prentice-Hall.

Henerson, M., Morris, L. L., & Fitz-Gibbon, C. T. (1978). *How to measure attitudes.* Newbury Park, CA: Sage.

Horst, D. P., Tallmadge, G. K., & Wood, C. T. (1975). *A procedural guide for validating achievement test gains in educational projects.* Mountain View, CA: RMC Research Corporation.

Krijcie, R. V., & Morgan, D. W. (1970). Determining sample size for research activities. *Educational and Psychological Measurement, 30,* 607-610.

Morris, L. L., & Fitz-Gibbon, C. T. (1978a). *How to deal with goals and objectives.* Newbury Park, CA: Sage.

Morris, L. L., & Fitz-Gibbon, C. T. (1978b). *How to measure achievement.* Newbury Park, CA: Sage.

Index

Ability tests, 44, 45
Analysis of covariance, 73, 94, 95
Analysis of variance, 73, 84, 95, 128-139, 153
ANCOVA (*see* Analysis of covariance)
ANOVA (*see* Analysis of variance)
Attitudes, measures of
  difficulties when used as pretests, 42, 43
  in time-series designs, 99-100, 102
Attrition, 62-63, 68-69, 82-83, 90, 102-103, 155

Baseline information, 34
Blocking, 39, 44, 143, 150-154
Borderline groups, 28, 156-160

C-groups (*see* Control groups)
Comparative information, 9
Comparison groups (*see* Control groups)
Confidence limits, 73, 84
Confounds, 29, 63, 68, 82, 89, 101-102, 109, 132
Contamination, 63, 68, 82, 89
Control groups, 16, 26-35, 56
  alternative program or alternative treatment received, 32-35
  borderline students as a basis for, 28, 156-160
  equivalent, 26-28
  non-equivalent, 26, 28-32, 88-90
  true (equivalent) 26-28
Criterion-referenced tests, 40

Design diagrams, 55-58, 61-62
Design implementation, 62-64, 67-69, 82-83, 89-90, 101-103
Design selection, 48-54
  in mid-program, 49, 52-54
  pre-program, 49, 51

E-group (experimental group) defined, 25
Educational significance, 78-80, 81, 83, 91, 92
Evaluation audience, 14

Experimental group defined, 25

Formative evaluation, 11, 14-20

Gains, 37-38, 40-41, 73, 94
Group defined, 25

Interaction of factors, 133-135, 138

Loss of cases (*see* Attrition)

Matched pairs, 154-156
Mid-tests, 45-47
Mortality, 37, 62-63 (*see also* Attrition)

Non-equivalent control groups, 26, 29-32, 86-88
  (*see also* Control groups)

Objectives (*see* Program results analyzed by objectives)
Outliers, 72

Post-hoc comparisons, 136-137, 139
Post-hoc matching, 94
Posttests, 35-37
Power of a design, 41-42
Pretests, 39-45
  of ability, 44-45
  for checking assumptions, 38-39
  for ensuring group comparability, 39-40
  for estimating pre-post changee, 40-41
  for student selection, 37-38
  to support the sensitivity of your design, 41-42
  when to avoid, 42-44
Program results analyzed by objectives, 74-78, 122-127
Programs with overlapping goals, 34

Random assignment, 140, 144-165
Randomization, 140-165
Random sampling, 140, 161-165
  stratified, 162

Regression, 38, 87-88, 89
Remedial programs, 20-23
Retention tests, 47

Sample size, 161-162
    table, 163
Satisfaction with programs, 22
Selection bias, 131
Significance
    educational, 44, 78-80, 84, 85-86, 95
    statistical, 70, 72-74, 79, 84, 86, 94, 95,
        132-139, 142
Special education, 20-23, 156-160
Standardized tests, 119-121
Statistical significance, 70, 72-74, 79, 84,
    86, 94, 95, 132-139, 142

Stratified random sampling, 162
Subgroup results, 85
Summative evaluation, 11-14

Testing effects, 31-32
Theory-based evaluation, 23
Time-series tests, 48, 58-61
    longitudinal design, 60-61, 98-100,
        115-116
    successive-groups design, 60-61, 98, 100,
        102-103, 116
Treatment group
    defined, 25

Unit of analysis, 140-144